UNCOVERING HAPINESS

SUCCESS

By Paul J. Toyle

To my wife Marie Martha Desormis, my son Kevin Toyle, my daughter Wendy P. Toyle and my brother Simeon Toyle

I can't forget some great supportive friends such as Michelet Josil, Zachary Evans, Frantzon Francois and others.

Table of Contents

Preface

Philippians 2:2-5 (NIV)

2 then make my joy complete by being like-minded, having the same love, being one in spirit and of one mind. 3 Do nothing out of selfish ambition or vain conceit. Rather, in humility value others above yourselves, 4 not looking to your own interests but each of you to the interests of the others. 5 In your relationships with one another, have the same mindset as Christ Jesus:

Apostle Paul, the one who wrote over two thirds of the New Testament book made an awesome experience with Jesus in their encounter on the way to Damascus and discovered how Jesus thought. Because of that, he was able to express it in the book of Philippians to encourage the Christians to think like Jesus.

Your thinking leads your body to go certain directions, does certain things and acts certain ways. In other words, your thinking may cause your failure versus your success. We see many examples of people who fail, not because they are bad people, but simply because they don't think right. At this point, someone may ask then, how should I think? Yes, we have the answer for you. You need to think like Jesus. Why? Because Jesus never made any mistake in His life. Is it not awesome? Yes, it's awesome because we need a role model to follow; Jesus is our role model. One thing about life, you have a price to pay for every mistake you make. I don't think we can afford making mistakes our whole life. And some mistake we make may cause us our life which means no time to make up for it, no time to even repent. Finding out how to live our life in the right way, which is directed by our thinking is crucial for our well-being and our future. While tremendous people enjoy the comfort of their life due to the result of the right thinking, countless people suffer serious consequences just for the wrong thinking.

My job as the servant of God is to educate the people base on the bible as to live a better life in Jesus, the Savior of the world. My friends, life would be beautiful if everyone took the opportunity to enjoy the thinking of Jesus and apply it to their own lives. There would be less people in jail, less misery on the earth, less spreading of disease, less sadness, less premature death, but rather, more joy throughout, more peace and a better future worldwide.

The fact is that Jesus' thinking reflects His personality. He passes the test of dynamic thinking when facing different situations by remaining constant and accurate in His work, his behavior and his action. If Jesus was one hundred percent man when living among us as declared by the bible, the contemporary generation should be able to imitate him.

After the bad experience of God with Adam and Eves and other subsequent representatives who failed miserably, God judged it necessary to send the perfect man, the infallible one to set the example for the human race, it was Jesus, the Son of God. God knows that man cannot inherit the kingdom of God without being born again and living a sanctified life before Him; He gracefully sent His only begotten Son as the sole example, sole way and sole life to be sacrificed for our sins so we can appear right before him. Discovering how Jesus thinks is crucial and imperative to be like Him and becoming one of the children of God. This book will teach you step by step in each chapter how Jesus thinks.

Chapter 1
Be Joyful

Philippians 2:2-5 (NIV)

[2] then make my joy complete by being like-minded, having the same love, being one in spirit and of one mind. [3] Do nothing out of selfish ambition or vain conceit. Rather, in humility value others above yourselves, [4] not looking to your own interests but each of you to the interests of the others. [5] In your relationships with one another, have the same mindset as Christ Jesus:

The mind of Jesus is joy. It's so painful to see how poverty invaded the world. From the third-world countries to the wealthiest one, we see people fight so much to gain their daily bread. It's also heart-breaking to see people suffer from all kind of illness, and nobody seems to care. At the beginning, man has never been made to be suffered to that extent. Man was created by God to be happy. That's why we find in the book of Genesis that God created everything that man ever needs to keep him happy. Why can't man be happy then?

After the fall, God is continuously looking for a way to make mankind happy by going through all kind of trials with them, using different dispensations described below until we are at the sixth one now which is dispensation of grace, but man is still not ready to enjoy the full blessing of God and be happy:

1. Man's Innocent.

This dispensation extends from the creation of Adam in Genesis 2:7 to the expulsion from Eden. Adam, created innocent and ignorant of good and evil, was placed in the garden of Eden with his wife, Eve, and put under responsibility to abstain from the fruit of the tree of the knowledge of good and evil. The dispensation of innocence resulted in the first failure of man, and in its far-reaching effects, the most disastrous. It closed in judgment: "So he drove out the man." (Gen. 1:26; Gen. 2:16,17; Gen. 3:6; Gen. 3:22-24.)
Salvation Gospel in this dispensation:

Do not eat of the tree of knowledge of good and evil.

Genesis 2:16 And the Lord God commanded the man, saying, "Of every tree of the garden you may freely eat; 17 "but of the tree of the knowledge of good and evil you shall not eat, for in the day that you eat of it you shall surely die."

2. Man's Conscience.

By the fall, Adam and Eve acquired and transmitted to the race the knowledge of good and evil. This gave conscience a basis for right moral judgment, and hence the race came under this measure of responsibility -- to do good and eschew evil. The result of the dispensation of conscience, from Eden to the flood (while there was no institution of government and of law), was that "all flesh had corrupted his way on the earth," that "the wickedness of man was great in the earth, and that every imagination of the thoughts of his heart was only evil continually," and God closed the second testing of the natural man with judgment: the flood. (Gen. 3:7, 22; Gen. 6:5,11-12; Gen. 7:11-12, 23.)
Salvation Gospel in this dispensation:

Do good and do not do evil, or love what is good and hate what is evil.

Genesis 3:22 Then the Lord God said, "Behold, the man has become like one of Us, to know good and evil. And now, lest he put out his hand and take also of the tree of life, and eat, and live forever"-- 23 therefore the Lord God sent him out of the garden of Eden to till the ground from which he was taken.

3. Man in authority over the earth.

Out of the fearful judgment of the flood, God saved eight persons, to whom, after the waters were assuaged, He gave the purified earth with ample power to govern it. This, Noah and his descendants were responsible to do. The dispensation of human government resulted, upon the plain of Shinar, in the impious attempt to become independent of God and closed in judgment: the confusion of tongues. (Gen. 9: 1, 2; Gen. 11: 1-4; Gen. 11:5-8.)

Salvation Gospel in this dispensation:

Believe God and build an ark.

Genesis 6:16 "You shall make a window for the ark, and you shall finish it to a cubit from above; and set the door of the ark in its side. You shall make it [with] lower, second, and third [decks]. 17 "And behold, I Myself am bringing floodwaters on the earth, to destroy from under heaven all flesh in which [is] the breath of life; everything that [is] on the earth shall die. 18 "But I will establish My covenant with you; and you shall go into the ark--you, your sons, your wife, and your sons' wives with you.

4. Man under Promise.

Out of the dispersed descendants of the builders of Babel, God called one man, Abram, with whom He enters into covenant. Some of the promises to Abram and his descendants were purely gracious and unconditional. These either have been or will yet be literally fulfilled. Other promises were conditional upon the faithfulness and obedience of the Israelites. Every one of these conditions was violated, and the dispensation of promise resulted in the failure of Israel and closed in the judgment of bondage in Egypt.

"The book of Genesis, which opens with the sublime words, "In the beginning God created," closes with, "In a coffin in Egypt." (See Gen. 12:1-3; Gen. 13:14-17; Gen. 15:5; Gen. 26:3; Gen. 28:12-13; Exod. 1: 13-14.)"

Salvation Gospel in this dispensation:

Believe God's promise.

Genesis 12:1 Now the Lord had said to Abram: "Get out of your country, From your family And from your father's house, To a land that I will show you. 2 I will make you a great nation; I will bless you.

5. Man under Law.

Again the grace of God came to the help of helpless man and redeemed the chosen people out of the hand of the oppressor. In the wilderness of Sinai He proposed to them the covenant of law. Instead of humbly pleading for a continued relation of grace, they presumptuously answered: "All that the Lord hath spoken we will do." The history of Israel in the wilderness and in the land is one long record of flagrant, persistent violation of the law, and at last, after multiple warnings, God closed the testing of man by law in judgment: first Israel, and then Judah, were driven out of the land into a dispersion which still continues. A feeble remnant returned under Ezra and Nehemiah, of which, in due time, Christ came: "Born of a woman-made under the law." Both Jews and Gentiles conspired to crucify Him. (See Exod. 19:1-8; 2 Kings 17:1-18; 2 Kings 25: 1 - 11; Acts 2:22-23; Acts 7:5152; Rom. 3:19-20; Rom. 10:5; Gal. 3: 10.)

Salvation Gospel in this dispensation:

Obey God and keep His commandments.

Exodus 19:5 Now therefore, if you will indeed obey My voice and keep My covenant, then you shall be a special treasure to Me above all people; for all the earth [is] Mine.

6. Man under Grace.

The sacrificial death of the Lord Jesus Christ introduced the dispensation of pure grace, which means undeserved favor, or God giving righteousness, instead of God requiring righteousness, as under law. Salvation, perfect and eternal, is now freely offered to Jew and Gentile upon the acknowledgment of sin, or repentance, with faith in Christ.

"Jesus answered and said unto them, This is the work of God, that ye believe on him whom he hath sent" (John 6:29). "Verily, verily, I say unto you, He that believeth on me hath everlasting life" (John 6:47). "Verily, verily, I say unto you, He that heareth my word, and believeth on him that sent me, hath everlasting life, and shall not come into condemnation; but is passed from death unto life." (John 5:24). "My sheep hear my voice, and I know them, and they follow me: and I give unto them eternal life; and they shall never perish" (John 10:27-28). "For by grace are ye saved through faith; and that not of yourselves: it is the gift of God: Not of works, lest any man should boast" (Eph. 2:8-9).

The predicted result of this testing of man under grace is judgment upon an unbelieving world and an apostate church. (Luke 17:26-30; Luke 18:8; 2 Thess. 2:7-12; Rev. 3:15-16.)

The first event in the closing of this dispensation will be the descent of the Lord from heaven, when sleeping saints will be raised and, together with believers then living, caught up "to meet the Lord in the air: and so shall we ever be with the Lord" (I Thess. 4:16-17). Then follows the brief period called "the great tribulation." (Jer. 30:5-7; Dan. 12:1; Zeph. 1:15-18; Matt. 24:21-22.)

After this the personal return of the Lord to the earth in power and great glory occurs, and the judgments which introduce the seventh, and last dispensation. (Matt. 25:31-46 and Matt. 24:29- 30.)"

Salvation Gospel in this dispensation:

Confess Jesus as Lord and believe in His resurrection.

Romans 10:9 that if you confess with your mouth the Lord Jesus and believe in your heart that God has raised Him from the dead, you will be saved.

7. Man under the reign of Christ.

After God's judgments on all the people of the earth, Christ will return to the earth with the Saints, and He will reign over all the earth for one thousand years. This is the period commonly called the millennium. The seat of His power will be Jerusalem, and the saints, including the saved of the dispensation of grace, namely the church, will be associated with Him in His glory. (Isa. 2:1-4; Isa. 11; Acts 15:14-17; Rev. 19:11-21; Rev. 20:1-6.)

But when Satan is "loosed a little season," he finds the natural heart as prone to evil as ever, and easily gathers the nations to battle against the Lord and His saints, and this last dispensation closes, like all the others, in judgment. The great white throne is set, the wicked dead are raised and finally judged, and then come the "new heaven and a new earth." Eternity is begun. (Rev. 20:3,7-15; Rev. 21 and 22.)

"This is the day the LORD has made; We will rejoice and be glad in it."(Psalm 118:24 NKJV) In the statement above, David clearly states that God has made those days for us to enjoy. We should never be sad and nothing should ever take our joy away. For one thing, as God reserves that joy to His children, in other to have that constant joy as declared in the book of Romans, we must be joint-heirs with Jesus as the bible said, "And if children, then heirs; heirs of God, and joint-heirs with Christ; if so be that we suffer with him, that we may be also glorified together. (Romans 8:17 KJV) To be joint-heirs with Christ now, we become the children of God as mentioned in the bible, "But as many as received him, to them gave He power to become the sons of God, even to them that believe on his name:" (John 1:12 NKJV)

It's important to know that the true joy is not something we can either buy, trade, exchange or steal from someone but it's rather a gift of God to His children. The fact it's been discovered and proved that joy keeps you young, makes you live longer, makes your systems function better and changes the whole atmosphere around you. There have been some theories on how to obtain joy, but it's never been more than a fable. True joy can be obtained only from God.

 Don't forget that God is the ultimate source of your joy. Don't make anything or anyone else the source of your joy; otherwise, when that thing or person goes away your joy goes with it/them. It's also very helpful to diversify your interests and activities so one thing does not consume all of your attention and focus. It is healthy to have a few things going on in your lives at once. For instance a career, a relationship, a hobby, an exercise routine, volunteering, time with friends; time to learn new things, etc. But don't forget that God is our ultimate source. "You have made known to me the ways of life; You will make me full of joy in Your presence." (Acts 2:28 – NKJV) The following are man's suggestion as how to be in joy:

Smile & Laugh

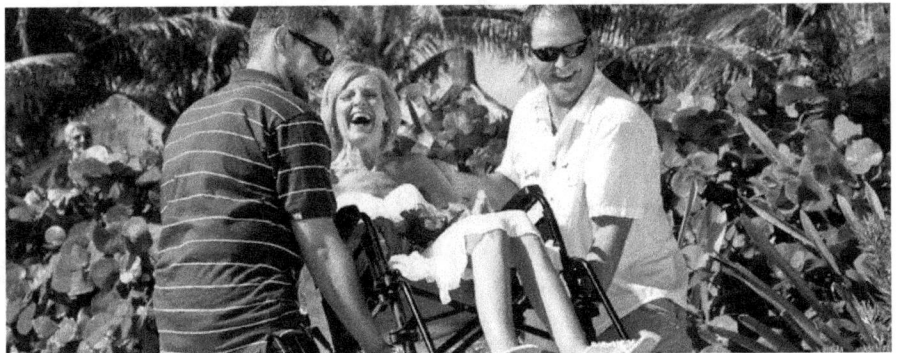

Smiling does wonders! If you want to instantly improve your mood, try smiling and laughing just a little bit – even if you don't initially feel like it. You will feel your mood get better, and this gets even more effective the more often you do it. If you're not used to smiling and laughing, don't worry, you can learn. Practice and work on laughing at yourself and at situations you encounter. If you make mistakes, learn from them, make amends where necessary, and move on. Don't underestimate the power of laughter and smiling – They are good medicine for the soul. Practice taking things calmly, try not to let things easily get to you. Are you smiling yet? You can do it... Smile :)!

Examine Your Thoughts, Refocus if Necessary

If your thoughts are constantly getting you down in the dumps, try refocusing your thoughts on things that will, instead, lift your spirits. Make a regular and conscious effort to fill your mind with and to think good thoughts. Remember, "...whatever things are true, whatever things are honest, whatever things are just, whatever things are pure, whatever things are lovely, whatever things are of good report; if there be any virtue, and if there be any praise, think on these things" (Philippians 4:8 – AKJV). Being stuck in a destructive cycle of negative thoughts can get your brain forming negative feelings like anger, stress and anxiety; which in turn make you get deeper into negativity. Refocus and reassign that energy to good thoughts, imagery and ultimately feelings instead.

Count Your Blessings, Be Thankful and Optimistic

Instead of focusing on the things you don't have, try to recall and be thankful for the things that you do have. Changing the way you think about and view things or situations can have such a huge positive impact on your life. You can make your life much more enjoyable by choosing to be constantly thankful for the things that bring you joy and happiness – for instance, your relationship with God, a loving and supportive family, wonderful friends, good health, purpose, hopes and dreams, hobbies, a place to live, a job you enjoy, etc. Make the best of what you currently have – always remember that you have something to be thankful for. And if there are things you desire to change, pray and work with optimism towards them – always one step at a time.

Make & Work Towards Goals That Challenge and Excite You

Strive for long term goals or dreams that get you going and give you something to look forward to. Goals that will challenge you and excite you, taking concerted thoughts, time and effort to accomplish. Something that will motivate you towards improving yourself, and that you can take pride and joy in. What do you want out of life? Do you like your current lifestyle? Are there things you would change? What makes you truly happy? How would you like to affect others? Think about it and pursue your dreams, but remember not to neglect important aspects of your life while pursuing those dreams – always try to find the right balance. Then work towards reaching your goals, one step at a time.

Put a Smile on Someone's Face

© BRAD PERKS #RC042

Do something to make others happy and you will reap the benefits by feeling great too. "And remember the words of the Lord Jesus, that He said, 'It is more blessed to give than to receive." (Acts 20:35 – NKJV). People who are ready to give tend to be a lot happier than people who are inconsiderate and selfish. Put a smile on someone's face. Making other people happy – whether they are strangers or people we care deeply about, can have such an amazing effect on us.

Take Time to be Sad When You Need to be Sad

Please remember that there is "a time to weep, and a time to laugh; a time to mourn, and a time to dance.." (Ecclesiastes 3:4 -KJV) We can't be happy all of the time. There are some times when we just need to go through certain "down times" – e.g. time to grieve, time to cry, time to heal, or time to express anger, disappointment or whatever "not so happy" emotions we are feeling. Life happens. Obstacles & disappointments will sometimes get in our way. challenges will seem to come from nowhere. It is all a part of life, and it is certainly very healthy to express those emotions (and act constructively on them) when the need arises. If we don't give our emotions a healthy outlet when we should, we are in danger of "blowing up" somewhere down the line. But the hope and prayer is that overall, we will be joyful in life, always learning valuable lessons when we are up and also when we have setbacks. Our hope, joy and strength comes from God after all, and "because He lives, we can face tomorrow"!

Forgive Others & Forgive Yourself

Don't allow yourself to be overcome by anger, hurt, grudges and revenge against people, life or God. When you release others and let them go, you release yourself to live life to the fullest as well. Accept people's apologies, even when they are not packaged exactly the way you hoped. Forgive. Move on. Forgive yourself too. Nobody is perfect, we all make mistakes. Learn from your mistakes, and move on instead of dwelling on them. Life is simply too short.

Develop Healthy Relationships

A basic need we all have as human beings is to have someone who loves and cares for us. Choose your friends very carefully. If your friends are treating you badly, have a bad influence on you or just constantly stress you out, then please, pray for and work towards finding friends that will have a good influence on you and also care about you. And make sure you are being a good friend too! You may need to look elsewhere and go out of your comfort zone to meet new people. One great way to meet people is by getting involved in activities that reflect who you are. Ensure any relationship you are involved in – family, romantic or otherwise, is a healthy one.

Stay in Touch with Family and Friends, and Have the Right Priorities

God is our number One friend. Don't forget to keep in regular contact with him just like you would an earthly friend. The more you grow in your relationship with God, the more you'll discover what an awesome friend he is. If you are married, your spouse should be your best friend (after God). If your spouse is not your best friend, take the time to pray and work on making that the case. Surround yourself with people who are positive, beneficial, encouraging, inspiring, motivating and helpful. Our friends should not just make us feel good, we also need friends who will lovingly tell us the truth to help us become better people when there is a need to (even when it hurts), not friends that will instead criticize us behind our backs. Maintain your relationships by keeping in touch, making an effort and regularly spending and enjoying time with your loved ones.

Rejoice and celebrate with each other. Support each other through tough or rough times. Be ever thankful for the friendship, companionship and love you share. Keep in touch, and don't forget to always show the people in your life that you care about them.

Explore, Go Out, Read, Sing, Dance...Have FUN!

Take the time to do things that you know will lift your spirits. Sing & Dance as often and as much as you possibly can. Put on some of your favorite uplifting music, something you know will get you in the mood to dance and sing (whether on or off key:) . Go out and have some fun with friends or/and family. Indulge in simple pleasures regularly. For instance, try to make time to curl up and watch or read something that will make you smile or laugh from time to time. You can read uplifting verses from the Bible. Read a really nice novel while munching on some yummy snacks. Enjoy life, rejoice, and be glad!

Relax and Sleep!

Seriously. Lighten up and try your best to avoid things that bring you stress, as stress can cause many mental, physical and spiritual problems. Take practical steps towards improving the things you can change and don't brood over things you can't control. Set aside time each day to simply relax and not have to worry about anything. Take vacations. Regularly take the time to relax with your loved ones too. And I cannot over-emphasize the importance of getting enough rest! Make sure you get enough sleep and rest regularly. Rest your body, and rest your mind. Wake up refreshed and ready to face (and enjoy) another new day, by God's grace.

Chapter 2
Love

Philippians 2:2-5 (NIV)

[2] then make my joy complete by being like-minded, having the same love, being one in spirit and of one mind. [3] Do nothing out of selfish ambition or vain conceit. Rather, in humility value others above yourselves, [4] not looking to your own interests but each of you to the interests of the others. [5] In your relationships with one another, have the same mindset as Christ Jesus:

The mind of Jesus is love. To understand what Jesus did, let's compare Him a little with the other earthly kings. When a prince is born, he receives all cares necessary usually from special people. He has the best maid to take care of him, he has the best health professional to watch over his health. He eats the most nutritious meal you can imagine. He is going to the best school possible. He can have whatever he wants, in other words, He never wants for anything. Basically, all he does is on his throne and reigns. Now the same king so loves the world, leaves his throne and comes down to live like an ordinary man and be beaten, tortured, scorned and crucified for us. Just to save the world. Is it not love? I declare that there is none like it. That's love........

God's love is most clearly seen in His giving His Son to die for us.

Jesus personally declares in the Bible, "By this shall all men know that ye are my disciples, if ye have love one to another." (John 13:35 KJV) Everyone at some time experiences some kind of love in their life from either a mother, father, sister, brother, friend or a lover, but never refuses to be loved; that means the taste of love is undeniable. Although love itself has been described in different ways and on different levels, it never loses its purpose other than to make someone feels good and happy. As Jesus mentions in the above verses that we should love one another, which means love should be reciprocal, and that's the beauty of love. Many people have turned off expressing their love just for the reason of not getting the love back in return. Let's look at the benefits of being loved versus the results of being unloved:

Benefits of Love

Sam Edwards / Getty Images

Ain't love grand? It's fulfilling, exciting and, as it turns out, good for you, too. We spoke to experts and found out that romance can bring you more than just giddiness—it can also positively affect your health and well-being. So whether you've been married for years or are single and looking, the following evidence will remind you why it's important to make room for love in your life.

It may bolster your immune system.

WE RECOMMEND

Research suggests that happy couples who engage in positive conflict resolution have higher functioning immune systems than those who don't, says Gian Gonzaga, MD, senior director of research & development at eHarmony Labs. He points to a study by Ronald Glazer and Jan Kiecolt-Glaser, in which couples were observed during disputes. The couples who displayed the most negative behavior during the fights also showed the largest decline in immediate immune system functioning. Those who argued in a more loving, positive way had higher immediate immune function. Looking to fight in a healthier way? According to Dr. Gonzaga, the key to positive conflict resolution is productively engaging in the conversation without retreating or "stonewalling" each other.

It can make you physically fit.

No, you don't get to bid your gym membership goodbye. But, it turns out that couples who exercise together have more success than people who sweat solo. According to certified fitness trainer and nutritionist Jay Cardiello, "nearly half of people who exercise alone quit their programs after one year, but two-thirds of those who work out with a loved one stick to it." Even better: Both men and women work between 12 and 15 percent harder when training with a romantic partner. Whether it's the excitement of being together or the extra push to keep up with your partner, sweating *à deux* clearly has its benefits. To reap the rewards, try scheduling gym sessions with your honey during a time when you'll both be able to commit, like in the morning or during lunch.

It might help you live longer.

"There's a long history of research that has looked at the health benefits of marriage," says Joseph Hullett, MD, psychiatrist and senior medical director for OptumHealth, Behavioral Solutions. "According to a 2004 study by the CDC, mortality rates were found to be the lowest in married couples." Dr. Hullett attributes these findings to the fact that, generally speaking, people experience less stress when they're in committed, healthy relationships—and less stress means better health. Plus, it has been shown that when men marry they give up some of their risky behavior—like heavy drinking and smoking—which leads to longevity.

That healthy glow of being in love? It's not just a myth! "When our love life is in order, our stress levels are lower," says Genaise Gerstner, MD, a New York City-based dermatologist. "There is less free-floating cortisol—high cortisol levels cause stress-induced acne—and thus less skin breakouts and pimples."

It can improve your heart heath

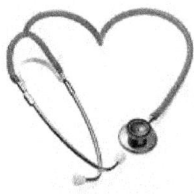

DID YOU DIVORCE YOUR IN-LAWS WHEN YOU DIVORCED YOUR EX?

"Human beings are social animals who have biological drives that make them want to find relationships," says Dr. Hullett. "When they can't find those unions, they're punished with stress." People in happy relationships experience less stress, which in turn improves their cardiovascular health. Furthermore, Dr. Hullett says people who aren't in stable, committed relationships have an increased rate of heart attacks, particularly those who have been widowed, giving a graver meaning to the term "heartbroken."

It can reduce feelings of pain

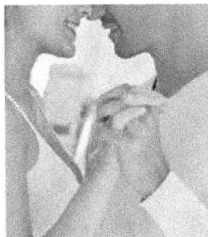

The comfort of holding your husband's hand can actually minimize your feelings of pain, according to a recent study. "Researchers studied people that experienced electrical shocks and found that holding someone's hand ameliorated the pain and perception of pain," says Dr. Hullett. The most fascinating part? These feelings of pain decreased even more when the female subjects—who were in happy marriages––held their husband's hands. "Yes, friends helped reduce the pain that these subjects were feeling, but their husband did a better job at it."

It can regulate your menstrual cycle

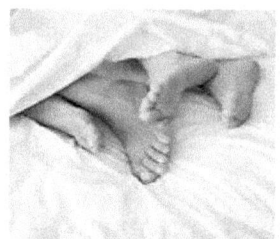

That is, love––as in *making* love––can. If you're struggling with irregular periods, try hitting the sheets. Eric Braverman, MD, author of *Younger (Sexier) You*, points to a study from Planned Parenthood demonstrating that women who have sex at least once a week have higher levels of estrogen and are more likely to have regular menstrual cycles than women who have sex less frequently.

It can improve your mental well-being

We all know that being in love makes us feel elated, but it's not just in our heads. There actually is scientific evidence of romance's blissful effects on the brain. Dr. Braverman references a study from Rutgers University that found participants, when they looked at photos of people they deeply love, had an increase of dopamine brain activity, which is associated with optimism, energy and a sense of well-being. Talk about being high on love! Helen Fisher, PhD, a biological anthropologist and author of *Why Him? Why Her?* supports this notion: "The bottom line is, the dopamine rush that comes from being in love gives you tremendous energy and optimism."

The result of being unloved

Being lonely in later life could be worse for your health than obesity, according to research. Feeling cut off from others can push blood pressure up into the danger zone for heart attacks and strokes, weaken the immune system and raise the risk of depression, a conference was told. The US researchers urged those in middle-age to think about how they are going to stay socially active in old age – and warned against retiring to the sun.

© www.alamy.com

Being lonely could be twice as likely to kill you as being fat. Research shows that despite the concern about obesity, feeling isolated and unloved is more likely to send someone to an early grave. John Cacioppo, a professor of psychology who has spent 20 years studying the impact of loneliness, tracked the health of more than 2,000 men and women aged 50-plus for six years. The loneliest men and women were almost twice as likely to die during that period than those who felt the most wanted and needed. Another study found loneliness to be twice as deadly as obesity.

Feeling cut off from others can push blood pressure up into the danger zone for heart attacks and strokes, weaken the immune system and raise the odds of depression, the

American Association for the Advancement of Science's annual conference heard. It can also disrupt sleep, leaving people feeling lethargic the next day and more likely to rely on sleeping tablets.

Professor Cacioppo, of the University of Chicago, has shown that we don't sleep less when we are lonely – we just wake up more.

It is thought that if we feel isolated were are extra-alert to threats and so wake up at the slightest noise.

Testimony of a girl who was unloved

I have been getting a lot of email lately with questions about feeling unloved or unlovable. Several people actually asked if I believed there were people that were unlovable. (The answer to that question later)

I don't think there is anything worse than feeling unloved. When I think of feeling unloved I think of feeling alone, hopeless and pretty miserable. I remember what that used to be like and am so glad feeling unloved is no longer part of my life.

I spent most of my younger years severally depressed. My last suicide attempt (25+ years ago) landed me in intensive care. When I got out of the hospital and looked at my chest full of needle marks from where they injected chemicals to restart my heart I knew it was time for some serious changes.

The biggest disease this day and age is that of people feeling unloved

Another unloved story

Whoever made up that rhyme is just plain wrong. Consider these comments from letters to Psych Central's "Ask the Therapist" column:

- "My folks just tell me that I'm fat and stupid. They're always telling me I'm no good." −14-year-old girl
- "No matter what I do, my parents criticize me. I get good grades. I help out at home. My girlfriend is polite to them. But I can never do things enough right for them." −17-year-old boy
- "Both my parents yell at me all the time. I try to stand up for myself but it only makes it worse. They say they wish I'd never been born." – 11-year-old girl
- "I think my mom is depressed. She stays in bed all the time. She expects me to clean house, cook dinner every night, take care of my little sister, and bring her whatever she wants. She's not a bit grateful. Actually, she complains about me to my grandmother and to my dad. Then they yell at me too. I don't think I can take it much longer." – 16-year-old boy

The anguish and bewilderment in these kids' voices is heartbreaking. Some of the letters are laced with anger. Most are testaments to the pain of feeling unloved by the very people who the whole world tells you should love you — your parents and extended family.

The teens who write are essentially good kids who are doing all they can to do okay in school and contribute at home. They try to please their folks. They often do far more in the way of housework and child care than is reasonable to expect. All they want is for their folks to love them but all indications are they don't. These kids want an explanation. They want to make it right. They wish and hope and dream that there is something they can do to make it different.

Sadly, there's probably not a thing they can do to make loving parents out of angry and inadequate adults. Their parents are too caught up in their personal pain or too unloved themselves to comfort and nurture their kids.

The true words for the kids out there who are desperately looking for love: you can receive it from God. "[16] For God so loved the world, that he gave his only begotten Son, that whosoever believeth in him should not perish, but have everlasting life.[17] For God sent not his Son into the world to condemn the world; but that the world through him might be saved." (John 3:16-17 KJV) God is so great in his creation, for every problem not only he created a solution, but also he makes available an alternative. God, in his omniscience, knows man may suffer loves from others. Before that ever happens, he expresses his love toward man repeatedly to show them that there is no need to worry about people who refuse to show you love. Your father who is in heaven has a greater love for you.

His love transcends all human loves. His love is not a temporary one but it lasts forever. We can magnify the love of God in this verse when he says, "[31] What shall we then say to these things? If God be for us, who can be against us?" (Romans 8:31 kjv) this verse justifies the love of God as a reliable love. That's guaranteed!! If I want to express it a different way, I shall go that way, "if God loves you, who can hate you?" Nobody over the past millennium ever made such a statement-promise. One thing about the promise of God, it's true, you will live it and it will come to pass. Nothing that He ever said has returned void.

With God's tremendous provision for mankind, there is no reason for someone to live life unloved. Unless one keeps himself from being loved, love is knocking on the door of every one, it's up to you to receive it, and notably not any love but the love of God. Jesus is so well aware of the importance of love, he said to his disciples that He will leave them but He will send a comforter to continue showing them love. "[25] These things have I spoken unto you, being yet present with you.[26] But the Comforter, which is the Holy Ghost, whom the Father will send in my name, he shall teach you all things, and bring all things to your remembrance, whatsoever I have said unto you." (John 14:25-26

Chapter 3
Unity

Philippians 2:2-5 (NIV)

2 then make my joy complete by being like-minded, having the same love, being one in spirit and of one mind. 3 Do nothing out of selfish ambition or vain conceit. Rather, in humility value others above yourselves, 4 not looking to your own interests but each of you to the interests of the others. 5 In your relationships with one another, have the same mindset as Christ Jesus:

The mind of Jesus is unity. During the period ministry of Jesus on this earth, one of his messages that stood out to the people was unity. Jesus unites with the Father and the Holy Spirit. He had always talked about his Father indicating his attachment to the Father. Look at the conversation he had with his disciples when they asked Him about his Father:

"5 Thomas saith unto him, Lord, we know not whither thou goest; and how can we know the way? 6 Jesus saith unto him, I am the way, the truth, and the life: no man cometh unto the Father, but by me. 7 If ye had known me, ye should have known my Father also: and from henceforth ye know him, and have seen him. 8 Philip saith unto him, Lord, show us the Father, and it sufficeth us. 9 Jesus saith unto him, Have I been so long time with you, and yet hast thou not known me, Philip? he that hath seen me hath seen the Father; and how sayest thou then, Show us the Father? 10 Believest thou not that I am in the Father, and the Father in me? the words that I speak unto you I speak not of myself: but the Father that dwelleth in me, he doeth the works.(John 14:5-10)

The passage clearly states an unbreakable bond between Jesus and His Father. Jesus was so attached to His Father, He constantly communicated with Him in prayer. Below is a picture of Jesus addressing His Father in prayer.

Matthew 11:25-26

At that time Jesus said, "I praise you, Father, Lord of heaven and earth, because you have hidden these things from the wise and learned, and revealed them to little children. Yes, Father, for this was your good pleasure.

Matthew 14:23

After he had dismissed them, he went up on a mountainside by himself to pray. When evening came, he was there alone.

Luke 6:12

One of those days Jesus went out to a mountainside to pray, and spent the night praying to God.

Luke 22:32

But I have prayed for you, Simon, that your faith may not fail. And when you have turned back, strengthen your brothers."

Luke 22:41-44

He withdrew about a stone's throw beyond them, knelt down and prayed, "Father, if you are willing, take this cup from me; yet not my will, but yours be done." An angel from heaven appeared to him and strengthened him. And being in anguish, he prayed more earnestly, and his sweat was like drops of blood falling to the ground.

Luke 23:34

Jesus said, "Father, forgive them, for they do not know what they are doing." And they divided up his clothes by casting lots.

John 11:41-42

So they took away the stone. Then Jesus looked up and said, "Father, I thank you that you have heard me, but I said this for the benefit of the people standing here, that they may believe that you sent me."

Jesus wanted to convey the message of unity so bad, during his passage on the earth, He was able to make friends with the people to show them real friendship. He visited them, sat with them and ate with them.

Martha and Mary are visited by Jesus

Luke 10:38-42

Martha and Mary offered hospitality to their friend Jesus of Nazareth, a respected but somewhat controversial Jewish rabbi. Their house was near Jerusalem, and Jesus often stayed there. Mary sat and listened to him as He talked, but Martha objected to the fact that she was left with all the work. Jesus told Martha not to worry about small things, but to concentrate on what was important.

Martha and Mary ask for Jesus' help

John 11:1-44

Later on Their brother Lazarus was dangerously ill, and in desperation Martha and Mary sent for Jesus. He delayed coming, and in the meantime Lazarus died. When Jesus arrived, both Martha and Mary reproached Him for not coming sooner. But Martha also made an extraordinary statement of her faith in Jesus. He went to the tomb, prayed, and called to Lazarus. Lazarus came out, alive, from the tomb.

Mary of Bethany anoints Jesus

John 12:1-8

Martha, Mary and Lazarus gave a dinner for Jesus. During the dinner, Mary anointed Jesus with expensive nard perfume. Judas objected to her extravagance, but Jesus defended her action. She may have been at the crucifixion, which happened just a few days later.

An overview of *The Last Supper:* Jesus sat in the middle of a table with His friends all around him, fellowshipped with them symbolizing that they ate his body and drank his blood in remembrance of Him. This indicates clearly that Jesus deeply believes in relationships. Just like He was united with the Father in heaven, He also wanted the same relationship with mankind.

Corinthians (11:23-26 NKJV)

23 For I received from the Lord that which I also delivered to you: that the Lord Jesus on the *same* night in which He was betrayed took bread; 24 and when He had given thanks, He broke *it* and said, "Take, eat;[a] this is My body which is broken[b] for you; do this in remembrance of Me." 25 In the same manner *He* also *took* the cup after supper, saying, this cup is the new covenant in My blood. This do, as often as you drink *it,* in remembrance of Me.26 For as often as you eat this bread and drink this cup, you proclaim the Lord's death till He comes.

After all the teachings received from Jesus Himself through the Bible, it's imperative for us to live as being one in spirit and of one mind. Whether we're talking about a sport team, work team, school team, health care team, church team, or home based business team, it's essential that we get everyone on the bus and moving in the right direction with a shared vision, focus, purpose and direction. When a team comes together they are more able to succeed together.

But if unity is so important then why aren't more teams united you might ask? Why are there so few great teams and so many average and dysfunctional teams? The answer is simple. It's not easy to bring people together. Agendas, egos, politics, power struggles, negativity, energy vampires, poor leadership, mismanagement, complaining, and a lack of vision, focus and purpose all prevent a team from uniting and performing at their highest level.

The bad news is that there are hundreds of negative forces and factors that can sabotage your organization, teamwork, unity and success. The good news is that unified teams show us it is possible to overcome them.

Unity happens when leaders are committed to and engaged in the process of building a united, winning team benefitting all. And if Jesus is our leader, He does just exactly that. It requires focus, time, and energy. Unity occurs when team members care more about the vision, purpose and health of the organization than they do their own personal agenda. And Unity results when you weed out the negativity that sabotages the basic teaching concept of the Bible as to how we must unite. Changing the mindset is essential. Unity happens when each person on the team can clearly see how their personal vision and effort contributes to the overall vision and success of the group. This involves meaningful conversations. Jesus stresses the importance of unity repeatedly in the Bible:

Matthew 12:25 (KJV)

25 And Jesus knew their thoughts, and said unto them, every kingdom divided against itself is brought to desolation; and every city or house divided against itself shall not stand:

John 15:5King James Version (KJV)

5 I am the vine, ye are the branches: He that abideth in me, and I in him, the same bringeth forth much fruit: for without me ye can do nothing.

After God creates Adam, He has seen the necessity for man not to be alone and then created a soul mate and united them to live together.

Genesis 2:18 (KJV)

18 And the LORD God said, It is not good that the man should be alone; I will make him a help meet for him.

The importance of unity has been preached in most places and institutions. At church, the word unity may be exhaustive due to so many sermons being preached in this regard. One of the powerful verses often use to convince people to stay together can be found in the book of Matthew when Jesus stresses it, "For when two or three are gathered together in my name, there I am in the midst of them."(Matthew 18:20) As Jesus units with the Father and the Holy Spirit, He wants us to be one in spirit as well. If we want to feel the presence of God in our lives, if we want Jesus to move faster to be among us, the best thing to do is to be among other people when we invoke him, pray to him and worship him.

At school, students look for peers to be friend with. They know that standing alone will not be the right choice for them. They need each other to talk. They need each other to joke. They need each other to giggle and most importantly, they need each other to exchange ideas and do work assignments. Studies reveal that when the student work together, they learn better and faster. That's why most of the schools implement the technique to assign students work to do together in class and out of class. Significant projects and lab work have been assigned to students in high school and college with the sole purpose of developing their knowledge with the help of others.

In sport, teamwork is highly recommended. A team that has selfish players is more likely to lose a game than a team on which the players rely on each other for performance. It takes the effort of the entire team to make a big win. One player may be better than another or the rest of the team but one player only cannot make a team win alone. During the game, either in routine practice or play in a championship, the coach always stresses playing together.

At home, parents always suggest to kids to stick together. When one is caught up in a fight, the other is expected to help. The elder child is usually taught to support the youngest. We see brothers and sisters support other siblings. Some people do exceptional things for their families. They suffer for them, sometimes in a hard way. Some give a part of their body (kidney, bone marrow, etc.) to implant for the other one to survive. Some offer support by paying food, rent, school, car and/or expenses.

God called us to live together in one spirit, one mind. No matter how long you may live, you'll never stop learning. Every minute of every day brings new opportunities to learn something we've never known before. As long as we're open to receive, God will continue to teach us every day.

In the current state of Christianity, how can we achieve virtually that we are one family and one body? Today, as in all the time, it is only possible to the extent or is kept "the unity of the Spirit". This unit cannot be broken, because there will always remain true that "we have all been baptized of one spirit to be one body" (1 Cor. 12:13), but it may well not be "kept". Also, Ephesians 4:1 to 3 urges us "to walk in a manner worthy of the call to which we have been called; with all humility and gentleness, with long suffering, we supporting one another in love; we *apply to keep* the unity of the Spirit in the bond of peace". Of brothers who do not "keep the unity of the Spirit", although they can taste some joys in common and the favor of a rally, they will not know the joys of the (Ps. 133), Nor to meet according to (1 Cor. 10:17)

What is of God in the family of God

The family we mainly present the side of the love and affection: they are bonds of affection which unite the members of a family. When the relations are according to the normal order of things, this affection is then shown and felt by all. Children of God, having received the divine life by faith in Jesus, "having believed ", we have been "sealed of the Holy Spirit"; we received "the spirit of adoption, whereby we cry: Abba, Father!" and we have access to the Father by one Spirit" (John 1:12, 13 ; 8:31 ; Eph. 1:13 ; Rom. 8:14 to 17; Eph. 2:18). We are loved by the Father, of a love which John 5:23 gives us a

35

measure and which we can enjoy already because the Lord makes us know the name of the Father, his person, his love, by the Holy Spirit that he has sent here (John 5:26 ; 16:7). The Father loves us as He loves the Son, and the Son, as the Father loves him; as children of the same family, we are urged to love each other in this same love, " poured out into our hearts by the Holy Spirit who has been given to us" (John 5:23 ; 15:9 ; 1:34 ; Rom. 5:5).

Without doubt, the father wants his children to have love always between them, that those who obey never cease to love their brothers, even their brothers engaged in a path of disobedience; but the brotherly love cannot be expressed otherwise than according to the teaching of 1 John 5:2: "By this we know that we love the children of God, that is when we love God and that we obey His commandments". The evidence of the love of a child in obedience, with respect to the one who does not obey, therefore is not in an association with him in his disobedience, but in obedience to the will of the Father.

The exhortation which is given to us is not having to keep the unit of the family at the price of a disobedience, but we "apply to keep the unity of the Spirit" (Eph. 4:3). The Spirit of God can only have a thought ; so that if the children are disunited because they have different views to the point of no longer being able to live together, it is certainly because of what some of them have stopped listening to the voice of the Spirit and are guided by our own thoughts. When everybody is trying to assert his personal feelings, the quarrels ensue, the "bond of peace", which must tighten in all members of the family, is broken the unity of the Spirit.

In a divorced family, there may be a few children who are suffering from a state of things so painful, and seek to address them. We have just seen, this cannot be that obedience to the Father's will. For what concerns the family of God, this will is clearly expressed in the Scriptures, and it is by the Holy Spirit that we can discern right and wrong. Would it be that two or three children who seek to know the will of their heavenly Father. For this we educate and lead by the Holy Spirit; they will have, for their part, found "the unity of the Spirit".

The "two or three" that enjoy such a favor will without doubt that the family is not in full; they will suffer, entering with sympathy in what the court feels fatherly, but be that as it may, they will enjoy the love of the Father, love which cannot be really tasted outside the path of obedience (John 14:21-26). They will show as well a love according to God in regard to their brothers from whom they must remain separated (1 John 5:2), and they treasure, with those to whom they can unite, the sweetness of the ties that bind between them all members of the same family. It is the fraternal communion according to 1 John 1:3, 4 and PS 133, "the communion of the Holy Spirit" of 2 Cor. 1:13 Together, they will worship the Father, as his family, because this is "the Father" which seeks to unite "true worshipers ", worshippers who" make worship by the Spirit of God" (Jean 4:23, 24; Phil. 3:3).

God sees, and we can see also, as the faith of Elijah considered the unity of Israel, as well the twelve stones to build the altar of the Lord (1 Kings 6:31 PM, 32). As 1 Corinthians 10:16 AM, 17 ; 12 and 14 teach us, it is as members of the Body of Christ that we can gather around Him, at the Table of the Lord - according to God, there is no other gathering than that - recalling that "we, who are many, are one bread, one body, because we all participate in one and the same bread". When the apostle wrote: "we, who are many ... ", Is it only the "two or three" which directed by the Holy Spirit, are assembled there as members of the Body of Christ? These "two or three" embrace in their thoughts all true believers, members of the only body where they are located, and are gathered at the Table of the Lord as an expression of the Body of Christ, which they proclaim the indestructible unit. Gathered in a locality, they represent the Body of Christ in this place, as did formerly the believers of Corinth in this city (cf. 1 Cor. 12:27).

Without doubt, several members of the body are not where, would be their place. Does that detract from the unity of the Body? Absolutely not. The family is disintegrating, which means, the fraternal relations exist, with a certain degree of communion, but which does not go so far as to allow these believers to find themselves together at the Table of the Lord, because "the unity of the Spirit" has not been "kept"; however "the body is sound in faith and without blame in their practice.

37

The fact of the absence of several members, the functioning of the body as a whole, in the gathering of believers is an expression of the assembled Body of Christ is not what it should be. There is not a harmony which would characterize the exercise of the functions of all of the members of the body if each occupied the place which is the Siena and was "useful" in its place. Perhaps there are some who do not work at all (even among those who occupy their place!) and who, therefore, are being depleted, which is a cause of suffering for the whole body and a hindrance to its development; perhaps there are others that work, but not to the place where they should, ignoring or losing sight that they have an assigned place and a service to fill in the body, with a view to the building of the assembly.

The Spirit is the Holy Spirit, His service is to exalt Christ and to separate the believer of everything which is opposed to Christ. To walk in the evil or retain a false doctrine, or even join those who are doing so is incompatible with the communion of the Holy Spirit. If the unity of the Spirit is according to the holiness, it is also according to the truth: this is not that which would result from the acceptance, by all the members of a grouping of the same profession of faith, but the one which arises from the acceptance of the truth of God, as we used to understand John 4:13: "But when that one, the Spirit of truth, is come, he will guide you into all truth." (1 John 5 :6: "The Spirit is the truth").

To ensure that the unity of the Spirit can be "kept", it must be that each teaches and leads by the Spirit of God; when it is so, all the differences are fading, there is only a thought, that of the mind. Because the truth is one, the Spirit of God cannot give two different lessons: it cannot tell the few that the unity of the body is proclaimed at the Table of the Lord, according to 1 Cor. 10:17, and the other, that, given the state of Christianity today, this unit is unworkable; it cannot not more teach to some that it is necessary to "withdraw from the unfairness", in obedience to 2 Tim. 2:19 AM, and to others, that we can be in communion with all believers, regardless of their conduct or the doctrine they retain, because they are children of God and members of the Body of Christ. Because "the Spirit is the truth", his teaching may not differ from that of the Word of God, which is also "the truth", and it is by the Holy Spirit that we can enter into the knowledge of what God wants to reveal to us by His Word (1 John 5:6; John 5:17 ; 1 Cor. 2:10-16).

The unit and the union are two different things. As we have already said, as to the unity of the family, the unity of the body is not to be done, they exist and can only be destroyed; while the union, left to the responsibility of the children of God, has not been carried out, except a very short time, all at the beginning of the history of the Church, as we have seen in the passages cited from Acts 2 and 4. There can be no real union, manifesting the unity of the family and of the body, that if God is the center; it must therefore be carried out necessarily, on a land of separation from evil.

The separation of evil is the first element of the union according to God. Would it not rather be that of good and evil, in trying to reach a goal which seems to be an excellent thing in itself, we in fact worked, unconsciously, to the ruin of a testimony according to God? In his testimony to the unity of the body, as also elsewhere in the unity of the family, and which can only be done in the separation of evil, in obedience to 2 Tim. 2:19. The union is something that is so valuable and desirable that there is sometimes prepared to well abandonment to try to obtain at least a certain external union: on the pretext of brotherly love, it would happen fairly easily on the moral evil, more easily still on the doctrinal evil, and it would work even in communion with those who practice or tolerate! "The Lord knows those who are his own ", though consoling, but "that it be pulled out of the unfairness, anyone who pronounced the name of the Lord".

I'm still learning, and I know I always will be. What God teaches me every day about unity continues to change my life. I've come to the place where I can honestly say, "Lord, eliminate everything in my life that's holding me back. Please take away anything that's keeping me from walking in unity and finding true fulfillment in my life." In other words, "Lord, reduce me to unit with my brothers and sisters—bring me to a state or condition of walking in unity completely!"

The great news is that I don't write this based on theory but rather from experience having witnessed the process of unification in countless organizations. I have heard from CEO's who have increased their productivity and performance by 30% due to the process of unification. I have heard from hospitals who say they can tell which members of their staff are on the bus and who is off the bus. I have heard from principals of schools who said their morale and unity were at an all-time high. I've received emails from customer service teams that have won company-wide awards for their teamwork, results and positive energy. It's truly a rewarding feeling to bring people together and best of all it leads to positive results. I wish that for you, your team, your family and your country.

Chapter 4
Generosity

Philippians 2:2-5 (NIV)

[2] then make my joy complete by being like-minded, having the same love, being one in spirit and of one mind. [3] Do nothing out of selfish ambition or vain conceit. Rather, in humility value others above yourselves, [4] not looking to your own interests but each of you to the interests of the others. [5] In your relationships with one another, have the same mindset as Christ Jesus:

The mind of Jesus is generosity. Jesus is so generous, I would never be able to finish explaining in this book all the facts that contribute to His generosity. In part, let's look at some generous characteristics:

Jesus Gave His life for all

The human race fails big time before God. Everything that's been done to repair the relationship between God and man has failed miserably. One of the main reasons we are living is to fellowship with God. Adam and Eve destroyed that relationship and it has never been repaired since. Jesus sat on his throne with his father and saw the struggle and suffering of man. He took the form of a man and offered himself as the Lamb to be sacrificed to redeem the world. There is none like it. The greatest gift the world ever received. Imagine someone who falls into a deep hole and stays there for some time. Everything that has been done to remove that person from the dark hole has been unsuccessful. And suddenly, someone just jumps into that hole and removes that person from that ordeal. What would be your reaction toward that rescuer? Does He deserve some recognition, honor, glory? He did that without looking for any glorification for Himself but for the Father in heaven can be glorified. When we think about how Jesus died, he did more than that. Not only did He rescue people out of the hole, He accepted being mistreated, crucified and dying for you so you can live.

Jesus provided wine at the wedding in Cana

Jesus performed his first public miracle at a wedding reception when they ran out of wine. Jesus made the water turn into wine and everyone was able to drink enough wine to satisfy their thirst. "And the third day there was a marriage in Cana of Galilee; and the mother of Jesus was there:² And both Jesus was called, and his disciples, to the marriage.³ And when they wanted wine, the mother of Jesus saith unto him, They have no wine.⁴ Jesus saith unto her, Woman, what have I to do with thee? mine hour is not yet come. ⁵ His mother saith unto the servants, Whatsoever he saith unto you, do it. ⁶ And there were set there six waterpots of stone, after the manner of the purifying of the Jews, containing two or three firkins apiece. ⁷ Jesus saith unto them, Fill the waterpots with water. And they filled them up to the brim.⁸ And he saith unto them, Draw out now, and bear unto the governor of the feast. And they bare it. ⁹ When the ruler of the feast had tasted the water that was made wine, and knew not whence it was: (but the servants which drew the water knew;) the governor of the feast called the bridegroom,¹⁰ And saith unto him, Every man at the beginning doth set forth good wine; and when men have well drunk, then that which is worse: but thou hast kept the good wine until now.[11] This beginning of miracles did Jesus in Cana of Galilee, and manifested forth his glory; and his disciples believed on him." (John 2:1-11 KJV)

Jesus feeds five thousand people at once

While Jesus was ministering, His followers became hungry. Jesus took five loaves and two small fish, blessed them and fed the whole crowd, and people found enough to take home. "6 Some time after this, Jesus crossed to the far shore of the Sea of Galilee (that is, the Sea of Tiberias), 2 and a great crowd of people followed him because they saw the sign she had performed by healing the sick. 3 Then Jesus went up on a mountainside and sat down with His disciples. 4 The Jewish Passover Festival was near.5 When Jesus looked up and saw a great crowd coming toward him, he said to Philip,"Where shall we buy bread for these people to eat?" 6 He asked this only to test him, for he already had in mind what he was going to do.7 Philip answered him, "It would take more than half a year's wages[a] to buy enough bread for each one to have a bite!"8 Another of his disciples, Andrew, Simon Peter's brother, spoke up, 9 "Here is a boy with five small barley loaves and two small fish, but how far will they go among so many?"10 Jesus said, "Have the people sit down." There was plenty of grass in that place, and they sat down (about five thousand men were there). 11 Jesus then took the loaves, gave thanks, and distributed to those who were seated as much as they wanted. He did the same with the fish.12 When they had all had enough to eat, he said to his disciples, "Gather the pieces that are left over. Let nothing be wasted." 13 So they gathered them and filled twelve baskets with the pieces of the five barley loaves left over by those who had eaten.14 After the people saw the sign Jesus performed, they began to say, "Surely this is the Prophet who is to come into the world."(6:1-14)

Jesus healed a man at the pool of Bethesda

Jesus can be remembered for His outstanding job in healing sick people. He has been
described as the greatest doctor of all time. No matter what kind of illness you suffer,
once you meet with Jesus, you must be healed. "After this there was a feast of the Jews,
and Jesus went up to Jerusalem. ² Now there is in Jerusalem by the Sheep Gate a pool,
which is called in Hebrew, Bethesda,[a] having five porches. ³ In these lay a great
multitude of sick people, blind, lame, paralyzed, waiting for the moving of the
water. ⁴ For an angel went down at a certain time into the pool and stirred up the water;
then whoever stepped in first, after the stirring of the water, was made well of whatever
disease he had.[b] ⁵ Now a certain man was there who had an infirmity thirty-eight
years. ⁶ When Jesus saw him lying there, and knew that he already had been in that
condition a long time, He said to him, "Do you want to be made well?"⁷ The sick man
answered Him, "Sir, I have no man to put me into the pool when the water is stirred up;
but while I am coming, another steps down before me."⁸ Jesus said to him, "Rise, take
up your bed and walk." ⁹ And immediately the man was made well, took up his bed, and
walked. And that day was the Sabbath. ¹⁰ The Jews therefore said to him who was cured,
"It is the Sabbath; it is not lawful for you to carry your bed."¹¹ He answered them, "He

who made me well said to me, 'Take up your bed and walk.'"[12] Then they asked him, "Who is the Man who said to you, 'Take up your bed and walk'?" [13] But the one who was healed did not know who it was, for Jesus had withdrawn, a multitude being in that place. [14] Afterward Jesus found him in the temple, and said to him, "See, you have been made well. Sin no more, lest a worse thing come upon you."[15] The man departed and told the Jews that it was Jesus who had made him well." (John 5:5-15)

Jesus healed a woman who had a blood problem for 12 years

A health problem that challenged all the contemporary doctors and scientists for decades, Jesus overcame it immediately. Jesus brought joy and health to a woman who had suffered from a blood problem for some time. One can imagine what joy and peace Jesus brought to the home of so many that He healed. We can say Jesus is the best doctor ever. There were no sick people who met Jesus and left unhealthy. Not only did He heal the woman with the blood problem, he also healed countless people who suffered all kind of infirmities. When people are desperate, they are willing to do anything. This indicates how desperate that woman was. She thought if she could only touch Jesus' clothes she could feel better.

"[21] And when Jesus was passed over again by ship unto the other side, much people gathered unto him: and he was nigh unto the sea. [22] And, behold, there cometh one of the rulers of the synagogue, Jairus by name; and when he saw Him, he fell at His feet, [23] And besought him greatly, saying, My little daughter lieth at the point of death: I pray thee, come and lay thy hands on her, that she may be healed; and she shall live. [24] And Jesus went with him; and much people followed him, and thronged him. [25] And a certain woman, which had an issue of blood twelve years, [26] And had suffered many things of many physicians, and had spent all that she had, and was nothing bettered, but rather grew worse, [27] When she had heard of Jesus, came in the press behind, and touched his garment. [28] For she said, If I may touch but his clothes, I shall be whole. [29] And straightway the fountain of her blood was dried up; and she felt in her body that she was healed of that plague. [30] And Jesus, immediately knowing in himself that virtue had gone out of him, turned him about in the press, and said, Who touched my clothes? [31] And his disciples said unto him, Thou seest the multitude thronging thee, and sayest thou, Who touched me? [32] And he looked round about to see her that had done this thing. [33] But the woman fearing and trembling, knowing what was done in her, came and fell down before him, and told him all the truth. 34 And he said unto her, Daughter, thy faith hath made thee whole; go in peace, and be whole of thy plague." (Mark 5:21-34)

Jesus changes people's lives

The good news about Jesus, no matter what is your social status is, He is able to fulfill you immediately. He would change your life for the best. I don't know anyone who can change people's lives other than Jesus. When they incarcerate people in jail as a punishment in expectation of a life change or a change of behavior, as the result, people are often getting worse than the way they were previously. I recently watched a television show called Forensic Files; after a man spent 20 years behind bars when found guilty in a murder case. Upon a few months after his release, he brutally killed other people. When he was interviewed, he asked the prison to never let him out again otherwise he would kill more people.

Zacchaeus climbs a tree in order to see Jesus

The rich man called Zacchaeus that the Bible describes was in a similar situation. He wanted a change of life. He had heard that Jesus would be around and determined to meet Jesus for a life change. He knows that no one else could do that for him other than Jesus. He pressed on to see Jesus and change came to his home; "1 And Jesus entered and passed through Jericho. 2 And, behold, there was a man named Zacchaeus, which was the chief among the publicans, and he was rich. 3 And he sought to see Jesus who he was; and could not for the press, because he was little of stature. 4 And he ran before, and climbed up into a sycamore tree to see him: for he was to pass that way. 5 And when Jesus came to the place, he looked up, and saw him, and said unto him, Zacchaeus, make haste, and come down; for today I must abide at thy house. 6 And he made haste, and came down, and received him joyfully. 7 And when they saw it, they all murmured, saying, that he was gone to be guest with a man that is a sinner.

8 And Zacchaeus stood, and said unto the Lord: Behold, Lord, the half of my goods I give to the poor; and if I have taken anything from any man by false accusation, I restore him fourfold. 9 And Jesus said unto him, This day is salvation come to this house, for so much as he also is a son of Abraham.10 For the Son of man is come to seek and to save that which was lost". (luke 19:1-10 kjv)

Jesus forgave the woman caught in adultery

Jesus is generous; he rather broke the law of the day to offer forgiveness to people. When the woman was caught in adultery, the very punishment that should have incurred was stoning to death. But Jesus views life in different angles, and always ready to offer something to the world. He is really our provider. That woman thought everything was finished for her. She thought that she had reached her final destination, the end of her life. However Jesus restored her life.

"1Jesus went unto the mount of Olives. 2 And early in the morning he came again into the temple, and all the people came unto him; and he sat down, and taught them. 3 And the scribes and Pharisees brought unto him a woman taken in adultery; and when they had set her in the midst, 4 They say unto him, Master, this woman was taken in adultery, in the very act. 5 Now Moses in the law commanded us, that such should be stoned: but what sayest thou? 6 This they said, tempting him, that they might have to accuse him.

47

But Jesus stooped down, and with his finger wrote on the ground, as though he heard them not. 7 So when they continued asking him, he lifted up himself, and said unto them, He that is without sin among you, let him first cast a stone at her. 8 And again he stooped down, and wrote on the ground. 9 And they which heard it, being convicted by their own conscience, went out one by one, beginning at the eldest, even unto the last: and Jesus was left alone, and the woman standing in the midst. 10 When Jesus had lifted up himself, and saw none but the woman, he said unto her, Woman, where are those thine accusers? hath no man condemned thee? 11 She said, No man, Lord. And Jesus said unto her, Neither do I condemn thee: go, and sin no more."(John 8:1-11)

Jesus raises people from dead

Jesus' generosity goes all the way to the point of raising people from the dead and gives them life again to continue their journey on the earth. It's clear that Jesus has no limit in the way He gives. Jesus offers the whole package without any reserve. Lazarus's death troubled his whole family and the neighborhood where he lived. That premature death refused to be accepted by his family. As Jesus has been preaching that He was the resurrection and the life, people believed that He could do something. This particular family spent time with Jesus receiving the teaching of their Master (Jesus). He proved to the people what he said could come to pass. He raised Lazarus from the dead and offered him an earthly life again.

"32 Then when Mary was come where Jesus was, and saw him, she fell down at his feet, saying unto him, Lord, if thou hadst been here, my brother had not died. 33 When Jesus therefore saw her weeping, and the Jews also weeping which came with her, he groaned in the spirit, and was troubled. 34 And said, Where have ye laid him? They said unto him, Lord, come and see. 35 Jesus wept. 36 Then said the Jews, Behold how he loved him! 37 And some of them said, Could not this man, which opened the eyes of the blind, have caused that even this man should not have died? 38 Jesus therefore again groaning in himself cometh to the grave. It was a cave, and a stone lay upon it.39 Jesus said, Take ye away the stone. Martha, the sister of him that was dead, saith unto him, Lord, by this time he stinketh: for he hath been dead four days. 40 Jesus saith unto her, Said I not unto thee, that, if thou wouldest believe, thou shouldest see the glory of God? 41 Then they took away the stone from the place where the dead was laid. And Jesus lifted up his eyes, and said, Father, I thank thee that thou hast heard me. 42 And I knew that thou hearest me always: but because of the people which stand by I said it, that they may believe that thou hast sent me. 43 And when he thus had spoken, he cried with a loud voice, Lazarus, come forth. 44 And he that was dead came forth, bound hand and foot with grave clothes: and his face was bound about with a napkin. Jesus saith unto them, Loose him, and let him go." (John 11:32-44)

Jesus promises he will take care of us

When we read the bible, we found countless promises that have been made from the Old Testament all the way to the end of the New Testament. As God was basically dealing with Israel in the Old Testament, He made promises to them, and most of them came to pass right before their eyes. Here are some of the promises:

Genesis 12 (TO ABRAHAM)

:1   Now the Lord said to Abram
       Go forth from your country and from your relatives and from your father's
       house to the land which I will show you.

:2   AND I WILL make you a great nation,
       AND I WILL bless you, and make your name great;
       and so you shall be a blessing.

:3   AND I WILL bless those who bless you,
       and the one who curses you I will curse.
       And in you all the families of the earth shall be blessed.

:4   SO ABRAM WENT FORTH as the Lord had spoken...

With the coming of Jesus in the New Testament, the world experienced a physical God who interacted face to face with them. They had a better understanding of God. His physical interaction led people to believe Him because he looked just like them and spoke the same language. Jesus promised the people peace, eternal life, freedom and love.

"25 Therefore I say unto you, Take no thought for your life, what ye shall eat, or what ye shall drink; nor yet for your body, what shall ye put on. Is not the life more than meat, and the body than raiment? [26] Behold the fowls of the air: for they sow not, neither do they reap, nor gather into barns; yet your heavenly Father feedeth them. Are ye not much better than they? [27] Which of you by taking thought can add one cubit unto his stature?[28] And why take ye thought for raiment? Consider the lilies of the field, how they grow; they toil not, neither do they spin:" (Matthew 6:25-34 (KJV)

Jesus promises he will come back to take us with him

Although many promises were made in the Old Testament all the way to the New Testament, if Jesus had failed to make us a promise, our hope would be in vain. Jesus has promised that He will come back to take us with him. Such hope and expectation keep so many alive, excited and hopeful despite what they are going through in life, they are resilient because they know that they have a better life waiting on them at the end. This promise transcends all the other ones due to the fact it could affect every one's destiny. People are always concerned about their future destiny. If people love to hear what their future is going to bring on this earth, which always lasts for a short period of time, they want to hear more about the eternal life that Jesus has promised them.

"Let not your heart be troubled: ye believe in God, believe also in me.[2] In my Father's house are many mansions: if it were not so, I would have told you. I go to prepare a place for you.[3] And if I go and prepare a place for you, I will come again, and receive you unto myself; that where I am, there ye may be also." (John 14:1-3 KJV)

The Bible states what God says with his mouth and his hands accomplish. And the Bible also teaches us that God cannot lie when He says, "[19] God is not a man, that he should lie; neither the son of man, that he should repent: hath he said, and shall he not do it? or hath he spoken, and shall he not make it good?" (Numbers 23:19 KJV)

Chapter 5
Humility

Philippians 2:2-5 (NIV)

[2] then make my joy complete by being like-minded, having the same love, being one in spirit and of one mind. [3] Do nothing out of selfish ambition or vain conceit. Rather, in humility value others above yourselves, [4] not looking to your own interests but each of you to the interests of the others. [5] In your relationships with one another, have the same mindset as Christ Jesus:

Jesus broke the barrier of self-centeredness by using the tool of humility. During the ministry period of Jesus on the earth, one of the things that stood out when he spoke was the fact that he always referred to His Father or his Father's will. He wanted to make sure that the people differentiated between Him and the Father, even though they are one God. He clearly showed His submission to His father. He respectfully places His father above Him. He never boasted about himself, nor did he behave as if He were the Father.

Jesus, the champion of humility

Jesus was the champion of conquering the world of egocentricity. His speech clearly conveyed His intention to be simply a messenger, but that does not stop people from worshipping Him. [One thing that needs to be emphasized, Jesus was sitting comfortably on the throne with His father and nothing could hurt Him where He was at. His Father made the decision to send Him to be crucified and died, and He obeyed Him blindly.] The suffering of Jesus was not a surprise for Him. He knew exactly what His Father sent Him to do in order to save the world. He humbly accepted it, "For God did not send His Son into the world to condemn the world, but to save the world through Him." (John 3:17) One can wonder how any child would react when he finds out that his father sent him to a mission in harm's way. The child would probably hate his father, or flee from his father or probably disobey his father from the beginning. But Jesus did the opposite; He surrendered Himself to His Father to be used according to His will and His purpose.

Jesus takes command and respects hierarchy

Jesus fully understood, acknowledged and accepted that God was above Him. He does not want to do anything outside of God's will; He shows great reverence for God. He does not want to offend God, rather He wants God to rejoice in Him. He stresses His feeling toward God in this passage when He says, "[37] All that the Father giveth me shall come to me; and him that cometh to me I will in no wise cast out. [38] For I came down from heaven, not to do mine own will, but the will of him that sent me. [39] And this is the Father's will which hath sent me, that of all which He hath given me I should lose nothing, but should raise it up again at the last day." This verse expresses a child that a father sent to accomplish a task and to be rewarded by his Father. He is not willing to lose anything that his Father has given him. He valued His reward because it comes from His Father. He loves his Father and appreciates everything that His Father has given Him. Consequently, when you love someone, you love everything about that person and everything that relates to that person. In addition, their interests become your interests, their joy becomes your joy and their pain becomes your pain. We can definitely say that God and Jesus share an unbreakable love.

Jesus bends down to pray to His Father

It can be very difficult to find someone who obeys his father just like Jesus did. Neither arrogance nor rebellion can be found in Jesus when it comes to obeying His Father; rather what we find is a complete submission. When it comes to doing His Father's will, Jesus behaves like a child who relies completely on His father for guidance and decision-making. When it was time for Jesus to die, He went to a remote area, fell with His face to the ground and prayed, "My Father, if it is possible, may this cup be taken from me. Yet not as I will, but as you will." (Matthew 26:39)

Jesus submerged under the water of humility, His will was not an option but the Father's will was all that mattered. Whether Jesus wanted something or not, he still had to put His will on hold and make a request. He went away a second time and prayed, "My Father, if it is possible, may this cup be taken from me. Yet not as I will, but as you will."(Matthew 26:42) He elevated His Father to the highest elevation. Jesus portrays himself like someone who has no power, at Gethsemane. He is empty of all power to live like a normal man to set the example for the world to follow.

During the last night of his life on earth, what object lesson did Jesus teach His apostles?

It is the final night of Jesus' life on earth, and He spends it with His apostles in the upper room of a house in Jerusalem. During the course of the evening meal, Jesus gets up and puts aside His outer garments. He girds himself with a towel. Then He puts water into a basin and begins to wash the feet of the disciples and to dry them off with the towel. He then puts on his outer garments. Why did Jesus perform this humble act?—John 13:3-5. Jesus himself explained: "Do you know what I have done to you? . . . If I, although Lord and Teacher, washed your feet, you also ought to wash the feet of one

another. For I set the pattern for you, that, just as I did to you, you should do also."
(John 13:12-15)

By displaying a willingness to perform such a lowly task, Jesus gave his apostles an object lesson that would be deeply engraved on their minds and would encourage them to be humble in the days ahead. The disciples were appalled by this action; one of them revolted and refused to allow Jesus to wash his feet. That indicates how pride is man especially when in a position of power. Jesus had to calm Peter down by letting him know that he will not take part in His kingdom by refusal the washing of his feet. From the beginning man has always struggled with the problem of pride. But Jesus' intention was to break that habit that prevents man to be all they are created to be.

We are born to be a servant

Man was created to serve, not to hold themself away from others. If Jesus can go that low, by washing people's feet, the question remains to everyone of how far we should go in serving people. The answer is clear; there is no limit in our task to serve others. If we have to be proud, we should be proud to be a servant. It's never been in God's plan to help pride, but He enjoys humble people's life when He says, "God resisteth the proud, but giveth grace unto the humble." (James 4:6) Man has to be honest with himself regarding what his pride. You can be proud of something that you have created, but what man ever created? Man makes great discovery by inventing with what was already created. Therefore, man cannot take credit that belongs to the Creator because He is the Creator of all things. Only God can be proud for what He has created.

When Jesus washed the feet of the apostles, it was not the first time he highlighted the value of humility

On an earlier occasion when some of the apostles showed a competitive spirit, Jesus set a young child beside him, and He told them: "Whoever receives this young child on the basis of my name receives me too, and whoever receives me receives him also that sent me forth. For he that conducts himself as a lesser one among all of you is the one that is great." (Luke 9:46-48) Aware that the Pharisees sought prominence, Jesus said later in His ministry: "Everyone that exalts himself will be humbled and he that humbles himself will be exalted." (Luke 14:11) Clearly, Jesus wants his followers to be humble, that is, lowly in mind and free of pride and arrogance. With a view to imitating him, let us carefully examine his example of humility. We will also see how this quality benefits not only the one displaying it but others as well.

In what ways did Jesus show humility during his childhood and his earthly ministry?

"When [Jesus] found himself in fashion as a man," wrote Paul, "He humbled himself and became obedient as far as death, yes, death on a torture stake." (Phil. 2:8) From his childhood on, Jesus left us a pattern of humility. Although He was raised by imperfect parents—Joseph and Mary—Jesus humbly "continued subject to them." (Luke 2:51) What a fine example that is for young ones, who will be blessed by God for their willing subjection to their parents!

As an adult, Jesus showed humility by giving priority to the doing of Jehovah's will, not His own. (John 4:34) During His ministry, Jesus Christ used God's personal name and helped sincere people to gain an accurate knowledge of Jehovah's attributes and His purpose for mankind. Jesus also lived in harmony with what He taught about Jehovah. In the model prayer, for example, the first point Jesus mentioned was: "Our Father in the heavens, let your name be sanctified." (Matt. 6:9) Jesus thus instructed His followers to make the sanctification of Jehovah's name a matter of prime concern. He himself lived that way. Toward the end of his earthly ministry, Jesus could say in prayer to Jehovah: "I have made your name known to them [the apostles] and will make it known." (John 17:26) Moreover, throughout His ministry Jesus gave Jehovah the credit for what he accomplished on earth.—John 5:19.

What was proved by Jesus' willing obedience as far as death?

Jesus Christ's course of humility and obedience on earth culminated in His death on a torture stake. He thus proved beyond a doubt that humans can remain loyal to Jehovah even when tested to the extreme. Jesus also showed that Satan was wrong in claiming that humans serve Jehovah for selfish reasons. (Job 1:9-11; 2:4) Christ's record of perfect integrity also upheld the rightfulness and righteousness of Jehovah's universal sovereignty. Jehovah certainly rejoiced when observing the unswerving loyalty of His humble Son.

What benefits have resulted from Jesus' course of humility?

Jesus Christ's life course of humility is a cause of joy and is highly beneficial. Jehovah rejoiced at seeing his beloved Son humbly subject himself to the divine will. The apostles and disciples were refreshed by Jesus' mild temper and lowliness of heart. His example, His teachings, and His warm commendation stimulated them to progress spiritually. Common people benefited from Jesus' humility because they became recipients of His help, His teachings, and His encouragement. Actually, all redeemable mankind will reap long-term benefits from Jesus' ransom sacrifice.

How did Jesus benefit from being humble?

Yes, for Jesus told His disciples: "Whoever humbles himself will be exalted." (Matt. 23:12) Those words proved to be true in His own case. Paul explains: "God exalted [Jesus] to a superior position and kindly gave Him the name that is above every other name, so that in the name of Jesus every knee should bend of those in heaven and those on earth and those under the ground, and every tongue should openly acknowledge that Jesus Christ is Lord to the glory of God the Father." Because of Jesus' course of humility and faithfulness on earth, Jehovah God exalted his Son, giving him authority over creatures in heaven and on earth.—Phil. 2:9-11.

Jesus will ride in the cause of truth and humility

Humility will continue to characterize the activities of the Son of God. Foretelling how Jesus will act against His enemies from an exalted heavenly position, the psalmist sang: "In your splendor go on to success; ride in the cause of truth and humility and righteousness." (Ps. 45:4) Along with truth and righteousness, Jesus Christ will ride in the cause of humility at Armageddon. And what will happen at the end of his Thousand Year Reign when the Messianic King 'had brought to nothing all government and all authority and power'? Will he display humility? Yes, for He will 'hand over the kingdom to His God and Father.'

If Jesus submitted Himself to the authority of God, why does man have a problem to do so? Despite the deity of Jesus, living with God on the throne in heaven before His incarnation, He fully submitted to God's authority. On the contrary, we find man not only refusing to submit to man's authority but also to God's authority. Are they better or greater than Jesus? Man needs to realize that humility is not a sign of weakness but it's rather a way to exercise power.

True humility leads us to be objective about ourselves; it enables us to recognize our shortcomings, our points to improve. It also allows us to recognize our forces, our talents, our qualities, without bragging, and in the purest objectivity, without trying to impress the other as well. Humility, therefore, is to see truth, quite simply. That is, to see on the path of personal development, of spiritual progress. On this path, we are in a position to appreciate what it has won, what it has learned, what it has experienced. We realize that there is still a lot to earn, that we are still shy of what we are called to be. All of this is encountered in the normal life. It is an interesting journey with beautiful personal challenges to meet. Here is some additional information that will help you to be humble in life:

Acknowledge your own mistake

We criticize others, because it's much harder to analyze yourself. However, this is not only counterproductive, but it also can become harmful. In effect, judging the others lead to interpersonal conflicts and prevents the formation of new relationships. Worse still, this prevents us from trying to improve. We are constantly judging the other, often without even realizing it. Try to do this exercise: each time you surprise to judging someone or a group of persons, please refer this judgment on yourself, and see how you appear. Try to correct your faults. Remember that the development and improvement are continuing processes.

Appreciate what you have

Let us assume that you are a graduate of a prestigious university and that you have finished among the first of your class. You deserve of course some congratulations for your hard work and your perseverance. However, there is certainly another person as intelligent and hardworking as you, except who has not had the chance to have parents like yours, grew up in an adverse environment or has simply made a bad choice in his life. You could have been in his place. You should always remember that a bad choice of yesterday would have been able to switch you entire life. Similarly, the good choice of today can change your life. Although you have probably worked hard to get what you have, do not think that everything is "won" and that you have the right to brag about your accomplishments.

Never be afraid to make mistakes

Being humble means to know that you are going to make mistakes. We all make mistakes. Understand this, and you will be getting rid of a very heavy burden. Each individual has only a tiny part of the huge knowledge accumulated over the centuries. In addition, our experience represents only part of the present, and we do not know anything future.

When you make mistakes, admit it.

Do not be afraid to make mistakes; that is fine. To admit that one has made errors, is even better. If you have made a mistake as a boss, parent or friend, people will appreciate the fact that you are ready to admit that you are not perfect and that you are working to improve the situation. Admitting your mistakes shows that you are not stubborn, selfish and that you do not think you are perfect. Admit your mistakes, and you will earn the respect of others, your own children or your work colleagues.

Avoid bragging

Don't brag about your achievements. If you are so formidable, people will recognize your efforts and will applaud you themselves. No need to talk about your super increase at work or the wonderful work of art that you just finished or the last marathon that you ran. It's true these things are impressive. But bragging will just seem egocentric and will have far less impact than letting the people admire your humility. This does not mean that you should lie about your achievements. All is meant to the glory of God.

Do not assign all merits to yourself

Okay, you have completed a complicated project at work. Have you really done everything by yourself? If this is the case, so much the better for you, but there is a good chance that another person has contributed to your success. Therefore, if someone congratulates you, say: "I could not have done it without "or" someone helped me a lot" do not brag about the way in which you have worked hard and all alone to achieve this task. Share the love. There is nothing more proud than to assign all the credit to someone who has not done it.

Enjoy the talents and qualities of the other

Look beyond your own person to discover people and the things that they are capable of doing or to simply enjoy them for who they really are. Please understand that people are different from each other and save the idea of interacting with different people. You will have your own tastes, the things you love, other things that you hate, but learn how to separate your opinions and your fear, to better appreciate others. This will make you more humble. Being able to appreciate the talents and qualities of others can also show you the qualities that you want to possess or improve.

Do not compare yourself to others

It's virtually impossible to be humble when one strives to be the "best" or to do better than the other. On the contrary, try to approach things more objectively. For example, instead of saying that Bob is the best guitarist of all time, say rather what you enjoy his music, or more simply, that you love his way of playing. Cease the simplistic comparisons, and you will be able to do things without worrying about whether you are better or worse than someone else. Each individual is unique. It's therefore difficult to say who is really "the best" in a particular field.

Do not be afraid of trusting the judgment of others

It's easy to admit that you made mistakes and that you have not always been right. It's more difficult, however, to recognize that others who are in disagreement with you may have reason. Yield to the wishes of your spouse to a bill that you do not approve. Sometimes, the opinion of your child gives you a different dimension of awareness. Instead of just saying you know that you are fallible, act accordingly. Of course, if you know that a certain line of conduct is bad, you are not going to follow it. Looking at it more closely, you may find that you are not always safe.

See the sacred text

It's another way to appreciate others. Consider the standards of morality and the proverbs on the humility. Pray to receive the humility and meditate on this quality. Do everything which is not to be egocentric. You can read the biographies, memoirs, the bible, documentaries on how to improve your life or any other thing that will help you to be more humble and to appreciate what others have to offer. If you are not a religious person, turn toward scientific thought. Science requires humility. It implies that you abandon your preconceptions and your prejudices and that you accept the limits of your knowledge.

Stay prepared to learn

Find people who inspire you in a particular area, and which you would like to be like. Ask them to mentor you. The confidentiality, the discernment and a good definition of limits are the elements necessary for the tutoring. Of course, you feel that you are no longer willing to learn. There is always something to learn in life. Taking courses in an area where you don't know anything as the pottery or the screenwriting can make you more humble. Just let others teach you.

Help others

Be humble implies respect for the other. However, a way of showing respect is to assist them. Consider the other as being at the same level as you and help them. It's the right thing to do. It has been said that if you help someone to learn or achieve, that's also your achievement. Help those who are in need will make you appreciate even more what you have, and you will be less proud.

Skip last

If you made the queue with friends, you must choose gifts or serve you food the last. Let your friends, your loved ones, the elderly or even perfect strangers, go before you and don't rush to meet your own needs. It is preferable to let others to be served first, you sit down and wait for your turn. Ask yourself: "do I really need to be the first to do this?" The answer will always be no.

Compliment the other

Praise another person, just for their pleasure and for yours. Tell your girlfriend how beautiful she is today, congratulate your colleague on his new haircut, or tell the cashier that you appreciate him. You can be more profound and praise someone for a beautiful aspect of his personality. Make at least one compliment a day and you will see even more strength of others. Start on the positive points of the others and not on their faults.

I am truly sorry

If you have made a mistake, admit it immediately, and acknowledge your wrongs. Although this costs prestige to ask forgiveness from someone, we need to swallow our pride and say that we are sorry. This will demonstrate to the person that she has value to your eyes and that you admit your error. Establish eye contact when you ask forgiveness in order to show that you are sincere. Your apology does not give you the right to repeat offensive actions.

Listen more than you speak

This is another excellent way to appreciate the other and to be more humble. During your next conversation, let your interlocutor speak. Do not interrupt and ask him questions as he continues to speak. Of course, you must contribute to the conversation, but get in the habit of letting the others express themselves more than you do in order not to give a bad impression. Do not just shake your head and say "hum-hum". Prove that you really are listening. Ask questions to show that you understand what is being said. Do not wait simply for her to finish speaking, thinking that it will finally be your turn.

Chapter 6
Empathy

Philippians 2:2-5 (NIV)

[2] then make my joy complete by being like-minded, having the same love, being one in spirit and of one mind. [3] Do nothing out of selfish ambition or vain conceit. Rather, in humility value others above yourselves, [4] not looking to your own interests but each of you to the interests of the others. [5] In your relationships with one another, have the same mindset as Christ Jesus:

The mind of Jesus is empathy. Empathy is the capacity to understand what another person is experiencing from within the other person's frame of reference. It is the capability to place oneself in another's shoes; Jesus did exactly that.

We are living in a world now where people become very selfish. They are looking for all kind of opportunities and spending tremendous amounts of time collecting earthly materials. It seems that the world revolves around them only, and they forget that others even exist. Their only passions focus on collecting all kinds of riches which can be far from satisfying their lust. The Bible taught and prepared us for the coming days when it says, "This know also, that in the last days perilous times shall come.[2] For men shall be lovers of their own selves, covetous, boasters, proud, blasphemers, disobedient to parents, unthankful, unholy,"(2 Timothy 3:1-2)

Jesus came to Earth to die for us

Jesus, on the other hand, forgets Himself, dies for sins that he never committed. Jesus had no interest other than saving the world. We find mom and dad who want to die for their kids because they are blood- related, or soldiers who want to fight and die for their countries because they are patriots, but we have never found a man other than Jesus who wants to sacrifice his life for the entire world with no distinction. Jesus has absolutely no interest Himself. All he was looking out for was the interest of others. Jesus does not tell us to do anything that He does not do, nor does He teach something that He is not capable of doing. He knows the level of strength and courage of all. He lives at the lowest level of manhood to understand everyone's concern. Also, He never tells someone to do something without providing the tools necessary to get it done. Why does man forget his teaching so quickly and engage themselves in the race to acquire material wealth? Do we forget that the life on this earth is temporary? For the Bible warns us, "19 Lay not up for yourselves treasures upon earth, where moth and rust doth corrupt, and where thieves break through and steal:20 But lay up for yourselves treasures in heaven, where neither moth nor rust doth corrupt, and where thieves do not break through nor steal:" (Matthew 6:19-20)

Recently I have heard something in news that was kind of shocking. A rich woman who was on the verge to die, donated millions of dollars to an organization to take care of dogs including building shelter for them. We don't have anything against dogs, but when we think about millions of people around the world who are living below the poverty line, that makes one wonder if dogs are more important than human being. This case has a similarity with the situation that Jesus found Him in two thousand years ago about the violation of Sabbath. Jesus rebuked them and said to them , "[11]If any of you has a sheep and it falls into a pit on the Sabbath, will you not take hold of it and lift it out? [12] How much more valuable is a person than a sheep! Therefore it is lawful to do good on the Sabbath."[13] Then he said to the man, "Stretch out your hand." So he stretched it out and it was completely restored, just as sound as the other." (Matthew 12:11-13)

Technology and Media

With the development of technology and the help of social media, news quickly spreads everywhere. To list some of them: people have access to news on the radio station, television, internet and etc. There is no excuse for someone to deny the acknowledgement of suffering that people enduring day and night due to the lack of financial ...By donating such amount of money to support dogs instead of human being can be viewed as a disgrace to the human race. Let's look at a statement that Jesus made regarding His people versus a dog when a woman came to beg Him for favor, " [22] A Canaanite woman from that vicinity came to him, crying out, "Lord, Son of David, have mercy on me! My daughter is demon-possessed and suffering terribly. "[23] Jesus did not answer a word. So his disciples came to him and urged him, "Send her away, for she keeps crying out after us." [24] He answered, "I was sent only to the lost sheep of Israel." [25] The woman came and knelt before him. "Lord, help me!" she said. [26] He replied, "It is not right to take the children's bread and toss it to the dogs." [27] "Yes it is, Lord," she said. "Even the dogs eat the crumbs that fall from their master's table." [28] Then Jesus said to her, "Woman, you have great faith! Your request is granted." And her daughter was healed at that moment." (Matthew 15:22-28 NIV). This biblical passage basically teaches us how to prioritize between human being and non-human being.

Man has never been created to live in a careless manner, but we were created to care for each other, to love each other and support each other. We cannot imagine how much Jesus emphasized love in His preaching during his ministry period on Earth when He states, "By this everyone will know that you are my disciples, if you love one another."(John 13:35)

What we see happening today is heartbreaking. People don't mind spending great amount of money on themselves for pleasure while we find people sick in every corner of the earth and unable to receive help at a healthcare facility. We find government spent unlimited funds to build nuclear arsenals that have the sole purpose of destroying people while, in their own country we can't count homeless people who have no place to live. To make it more appalling, in our churches we found ministers who buy private jets that cost millions of dollars while people in the church are continually praying to God for their daily bread. Is humanity having no more value to the eyes of others, or is the new generation lifestyle? Or perhaps we are at the end of time. For the Bible says, "[12] And because iniquity shall abound, the love of many shall wax cold." (Matthew 24:12) Nobody today wants to help others without looking out for their own interest or being complacent. At the government level, ones who have been elected to watch over the citizens and the good functioning of the country become so corrupted sometimes. People lose trust in them. Most of them take advantage of their positions to enrich themselves and do little or nothing for the masses of people who suffer. They forgot they were elected by the people and for the people. Instead of serving the community, they would rather see the community serving them. They drive luxurious cars that the tax payers pay for with no intention to create a way for a change of life. They travel to the country they want, often times in a private jet, while the mass has no transportation. During the election campaign, they promise beyond unreasonable doubt, while they know that their promise is uncertain. They swear by placing their hands on a Sacred Bible which often turns out to be false.

On the other hand, some who claim credit for helping others usually turn out to be family members, friends or someone that they like. It's obvious that some people who are in the position to help others are concerned only about their loved ones. Once their families and people they like work, eat, dress and live a good life, that is all it takes for them to be happy. People generally don't think outside themselves a great deal of time. It is a sad but simple truth that the average person filters their world through their ego, meaning that they think about most things in terms of "me" or " their loved ones". This means that, unless who you are or what you have done directly affects their life, they are unlikely to spend much time thinking about you at all.

It's glorious that we still have some people available to do volunteer works. The United States is at the higher rate of people among adults who dedicate themselves to helping others. There is simply nothing in society that says someone is mandated to help someone else. But in my last book, "How a Foreigner Can be Successful in America", I explained how the law of conscience works. Every person has the opportunity to experience this law in their life. It's not something you need to buy, or something you could work for to earn it, but it's rather a free gift from God given to everyone. Before people even understand the law that governs the society, they are already under a law which presents as a little inner voice talking to you and directing your behavior. That's the law of conscience.

Humans are born with an instinct to help others. No one has ever become poor by giving. When we look at the woman that the Bible describes as a poor widow, she is an honest and cheerful giver. She gave everything she has and accepted being penniless.

She had no expectation of money because nobody promised her anything, but she feels great when helping because of her desire to give. "[42] Then one poor widow came and threw in two mites, which make a quadrans. [43] So He called His disciples to Himself and said to them, "Assuredly, I say to you that this poor widow has put in more than all those who have given to the treasury; [44] for they all put in out of their abundance, but she out of her poverty put in all that she had, her whole livelihood." (Mark 12:42-44) Some people are waiting for their hand to be full of riches in order to give or contribute to a cause, but understand that they miss the great point of giving. We don't give because we have enough but we give because it's the right thing to do. We don't need to live in abundance to feel comfortable to giving.

I remember when I was growing up. It's always been a pleasure for my mom to give. Nothing could stop her from sharing her heart with others. She cooked food and she shared it. She had money and she shared it. She went to market to buy groceries, and she shared them. She sold products, and she shared some of them anyway. Although we were (the kids) mumbling about that, she still shared. As a result, her life has never been miserable. She is 71 years old, she is still working and she is strong like someone who's in their 30's. It's always been her honor and her pleasure to give.

In ancient times, there was a man who became famous because of news that circulated so fast in that neighborhood. Although there was no means of refrigerating food at that time, he claimed that he slaughtered a cow and spent one year eating that meat. Everyone was shocked and wondered how this could happen. As the people continued to wonder, one man decided to do the same to gain some reputation too or to prove to people that was nothing. He killed one of the big cows he had and seasoned it pretty good with salt and expected it to last for a year while eating it piece by piece. After three months, the rest of the meat spoiled and deteriorated so badly, no seasoning could do a thing for the continued preservation. He woke up one day and decided to ask the famous man what he did to conserve that meat for a year. The man decided to tell him the secret. He told him that when he slaughtered his cow, he shared it with the people in the neighborhood. Now whenever his neighbors killed their cows, they always sent him some. It takes him a year to eat all that meat. The man was shocked and realized that he was far from being successful in his quest.

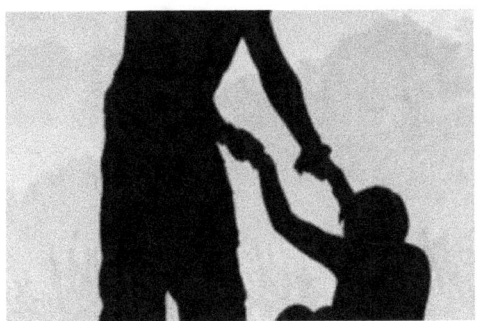

I have also heard that a man jumped onto a train track to rescue an old man who fell on the train rail while waiting for the train to come. We need to recognize and appreciate our heroes; he is our role model. He does not mind risking his life to save someone else's life. Life in society places on all of us a certain social responsibility, which implies, assisting a person in difficulty. In an emergency situation, it is possible that the rescuer or the "Good Samaritan " may cause injury to the person that seeks help . It is also possible that the rescuer may cause serious injury to himself or face death as a result of his intervention. But the fact that he knows that he has a duty to serve others, does not allow remaining idle to see a man die in his presence. To prevent his conscience from judging him, he must do something.

Generally, yes. The law requests to each citizen to bring relief to another person whose life is in danger. This obligation exists, for example, for any driver who is involved in a highway accident, but also for any person witness to a situation because of the dramatic consequences that may ensue.

For example: your neighbor collapsed suddenly on his lawn, a victim of a heart attack. You have the obligation to rescue him by calling the ambulance and helping physically.

Attention! You do not have the obligation to bring relief to others at any price. In effect, you can refrain when an intervention poses a risk to your own life or the life of other persons or for any other reasonable grounds.

Example: you arrive on the scene of an accident involving dozens of victims. After communicating with the emergency services, you help the victims most in need. Therefore, the wounded that you have not had the time to help could not hold you responsive.

Or even: you witness an accident or a car plunged into a river. If you don't know how to swim, you do not have the obligation to try to save the life of the driver by plunging into the river. However, you have the obligation to call for help quickly.

Helping others

It's a fundamental part of humanity, bonding together and helping a fellow man or woman. In times of tragedy, the stories of those who help others are inspiring, such as helping a nation recovers from national disasters and terrorist attacks. Some men and women even devote their lives to helping others, from the police force that protects our cities, to the fire departments who run into burning buildings, to the service men and women who risk their lives for the common good.

But helping others isn't limited to these grand gestures or times of tribulation. Helping others can be done each and every day. And contrary to what you may have heard, helping others doesn't always have to be a selfless act. No matter what the motivation, getting out and helping others is the key. Although it's not the intent of the book but it's important to understand that helping others can actually help yourself.

We can look at it also the opposite way. Many people spent time sowing corn, at the end of the season they want to reap beans. It never works that way. If you do bad, bad will come find you. But it works the other way, too. When you are a good person and help people, good things seem to happen. And while you may not believe in an inter-connected universe that rewards good deeds, there is something to be said about how helping others changes your perspective. When you're helping others, you will often feel better about yourself, increasing the likelihood that your next experience will be a positive one, rather than a negative one.

It's maybe the most cited benefit of doing good: you'll feel great. Helping others is a great way to feel better about yourself. Seeing a smile or even tears of joy makes it all worth it. Your conscience is clear and because of that, you can sleep well, live well and feel good.

People notice when you're doing good. It may not be the reason you help out, but someone is always watching. Even the simplest gesture can make an awesome impression.

As Christians, those who follow Jesus Christ- must show empathy to others. It's not an option but it's an obligation. Here are some basic suggestive ways to show empathy to others:

Eye Contact

This sounds so basic, but it's happening in everyday life. With the invention of cell phones on the market, most people are always busy talking with someone on the phone. Because of that, when you are talking to them, it's really difficult to have eye contact with them. This kind of body language says "I am more concerned with the person on the phone." That does not send any positive signal to be empathetic when you fail to maintain eye contact with the person who is talking with you. They want to know that you are listening to them. Ignoring someone when they are confiding in you is a HUGE slap in the face. When someone really needs you to listen, show them you care by looking at them. And most importantly, put yourself in their shoes so you can get an idea of what they are going through. They will believe that you care about them when you look them in the eye and try to understand their situation.

Engage Someone

Some people are super-shy and find it hard to vent to others. But, many times you can tell by their expression that something is wrong. A great way to show empathy is to approach them and ask if there is anything wrong. Let them know that you genuinely care about their situation and that you would be glad to listen and help in any way that you can. People feel empathy when others go out of their way to make sure everything is okay. And of course, always try and see things from their perspective. When you can see it from their eyes, they will know it. This will help them feel secure in the moment.

Meet the Need

People go through all kinds of problems in life. Some can be fixed while others cannot. If someone confides in you about an issue and you have the ability to meet their need, then consider helping them. When helping someone fix an issue they will feel like you understand their issue. It's another way of saying, "I get what's going on, and I want to help because I would not want this to happen to me either." This is one of the best ways to show empathy because it may very well be the memory that causes them to help someone else later on. Pay it forward!

Pray

Praying is one of the best things you can do with someone who is struggling. When you pray for someone, they will feel like you care about them. Pray specifically about their need and that God would give them peace through the trial that they are going through. Pray that God will be with them through it all and that if it is His will that He will use you in any way that you can help. Like the previous examples, it's really all about showing that you care for someone. You would want someone to pray with you in hard times and that is one reason why you should pray for others in hard times. They will understand that you are trying to understand their situation when you take the time to talk with them about what is going on and then pray about it.

Mourn With Them

When you cry with someone you are saying, "I am so sorry. I understand this hurts so badly. I want to be here for you. I cannot think of a better way to show empathy then to cry with someone who is sad. When you cry with someone you are saying, "I am so sorry. I understand this hurts so badly. I want to be here for you." They will see that you are looking at things from their eyes because you are feeling what they are feeling in the moment. And yes, men, it is okay to cry! God made us in His image you know! So, don't be afraid to let the tears fall when it is a natural act.

Helping others shall be a weight that everyone should carry wherever they go. If Jesus carried it for everyone and encouraged us to do the same, his message should not be in vain. It could never inhibit you from living your life, because your entire being (your personality, your thoughts, your actions) are controlled by a standard ideology of how God wants you to be. You can make a conscious effort to be more empathetic; to let yourself be what God wants you to be. It's a skill that needs to be practiced, like meditating. But once you truly understand how to do it, you will see the world as entirely different.

Chapter 7
Same Mindset in Relationships

Philippians 2:2-5 (NIV)

[2] then make my joy complete by being like-minded, having the same love, being one in spirit and of one mind. [3] Do nothing out of selfish ambition or vain conceit. Rather, in humility value others above yourselves, [4] not looking to your own interests but each of you to the interests of the others. [5] In your relationships with one another, have the same mindset as Christ Jesus:

It's provable that Jesus had the same mind set in relationship with the Father. The bond Jesus had with the Father is inconceivable. This union formed from the beginning and will remain constant for eternity. As you all well know, there's never been a conflict that existed between God and the Son Jesus, it's all about union, love and glory. The definition of the Trinity is commonly accepted as: one God in three persons, God the Father, God the Son and God the Holy Spirit. Among the biblical texts cited, to try to prove that Jesus and Jehovah are one and the same person, we found those who consider the Trinity.

For example, Jehovah said that it is ' the first and the last ', in Isaiah 44:6. However Jesus is designated by the same expression in Revelation 1:17. In all logic, there can be only one ' first and last ', right? Certainly! Provided that this expression has the same meaning for Jehovah and for Jesus ...

In Isaiah 43:11 Jehovah said: "Me, I am Jehovah, and outside of me there is no savior." Even though in Hosea (Hosea) 13:4 or Jehovah said: "But I am Jehovah thy God since the country of Egypt; thou knewest not of God, except me, and there was a savior that me." However, the Bible assigns this same role of savior to Jesus (John 4:42 ; 2Timothy 1:10; 2Peter 3:18). Therefore, since Jehovah stated that outside of him there is no savior, must it be deduced necessarily that Jesus is Jehovah?

In Isaiah 44:24 Jehovah said: "I, Jehovah, I am doing everything, I extend the heavens only me, I spread the earth. Who was with me? "And yet: " Me, I have made the earth and created man upon it. Me - these are my hands, have stretched out the heavens" (Isaiah 45:12). However, in Hebrews 1:10 the Bible said about Jesus: "thee, in the beginning, o Lord, thou hast laid the foundations of the earth, and the heavens are the works of thy hands." Then, Jehovah was He the only onto ' extend the heavens ', or not?

We learn in the Bible to worship God and God only. The bible describes Jesus being worshipped. To worship Jesus is to accept Jesus as God and having the same mind as God when the Bible says, "'As surely as I live,' says the LORD, every knee will bend to me, and every tongue will confess and give praise to God.'" The Apostle Paul called Jesus "our great God and Savior" (Titus 2:13), and points out that, prior to His incarnation, Jesus existed in the "form of God" (Philippians 2:5-8). God the Father says regarding Jesus: "Your throne, O God will last forever and ever" (Hebrews 1:8). The Apostle John says that "in the beginning was the Word and the Word was with God and the Word [Jesus] was God (John 1:1). Other passages identify Jesus as the Creator and Sustainer of the universe (John 1:3;Colossians 1:16-17;Hebrews 1:2). Jesus receives worship several times in the gospels (Matthew 2:11,28:9,17;Luke 24:52;John 9:38,20:28). Jesus is never said to reject such adoration. Rather, He accepts such worship as well- placed. In general the Bible portrays Jesus as fully deity.

Relationship in the church

The incarnation and the ministry of Jesus in the New Testament led him to establish His church for the saints to gather and worship God. He sets the example of how the church should be before He went back to His Father in heaven. All his followers should know that the church belongs to Jesus Christ because during his conversation with Peter he states, "**18** And I say also unto thee, That thou art Peter, and upon this rock I will build my church; and the gates of hell shall not prevail against it." (Matthew 16:18) And if you are his disciples then you should follow His example.

Jesus once said to His disciples if you love me then you need to do what I tell you. "15 If you love me, keep my commands." (John 14:15) when we look at the history of the primitive church, they were united with one accord. Today, things we see going on in the church are heartbreaking. God blesses a unified church. Many churches have tremendous potential, but they never achieve what God desires because the members spend all their time fighting with one another. All of the energy is focused inward.

The Bible talks more about unity of the church than it does about either heaven or hell. It's that important. Churches are made up of people, and there are no perfect people. So people get into conflict with each other. We need to learn how to deal with those situations:

1. Avoid situations that cause arguments. The Bible says in 2 Timothy 2:23-24 (NIV): "Don't have anything to do with foolish and stupid arguments, because you know they produce quarrels. And the Lord's servant must not quarrel; instead, he must be kind to everyone, able to teach, not resentful." Pastors should avoid causing arguments. You need to set the example for your whole church on this issue. When a minor argument comes along, refuse to get in the middle of it. You don't need to have an opinion on everything. Some discussions don't deserve your participation. Focus your conversation on topics that matter.

2. Teach troublemakers to repent. 2 Timothy 2:25-26 (NIV) says, "Those who oppose him, he must gently instruct, in the hope that God will grant them repentance leading them to a knowledge of the truth, and that they will come to their senses and escape from the trap of the devil, who has taken them captive to do his will." Most people don't like confrontations. But we can't run from them. You must gently instruct those creating dissention and opposing the teaching in the church.

3. Warn those causing trouble that their negative words hurt others. 2 Timothy 2:14 (NIV) says, "Keep reminding them of these things. Warn them before God against quarreling about words. It is of no value and only ruins those who listen." People need to know that their words have consequences.

4. Make a plea for harmony and unity. Paul did this in Philippians 4:2 (NIV). He said, "I plead with Euodia and I plead with Syntyche to agree with each other in the Lord." There were two very strong willed women in the church named Euodia and Syntyche who were causing so much friction in the church that Paul's plea for them to stay united is in the Bible. Fighting in a church doesn't just affect the combatants, but it also influences the whole church as people start taking sides. You'll need to make a plea for unity directly to those causing problems.

5. Rebuke with authority if necessary. Paul says in Titus 2:15-3:1, "These, then, are the things you should teach. Encourage and rebuke with all authority. Do not let anyone despise you. Remind the people to be subject to rulers and authorities, to be obedient, to be ready to do whatever is good." You may need to confront the contentious person as well.

6. Remove them from the church if they ignore two warnings. Titus 3:10-11 says, "Warn a divisive person once, and then warn him a second time. After that, have nothing to do with him. You may be sure that such a man is warped and sinful; he is self-condemned." No pastor wants to do this, but at last resort you may need to remove the contentious person from the church. You've got to protect the unity of your church. If that means getting rid of troublemakers, do it.

The Bible teaches that as the church grows, Satan will do everything he can to cause division. Even well-meaning people, even believers, can be used as tools of Satan to hurt the body of Christ. As shepherds of God's people, it's our job to protect our congregations from Satan's greatest weapon – disunity. It's not always easy, but it's what we've been called to do.

Relationship in the family

There is nothing more beautiful than a family union. When we look at the word family in depth, we see resemblance, same image, relationship, union, same purpose, common ground and all the knits. The family should also include that we are real. We all made mistakes, and learned. We all say sorry, we forgive and give second chances. We laugh, we have fun, and we give each other a hug when it's needed and most of all, we love each other unconditionally. Our home should be a place where we will always belong, no matter what.

In contrast, what we find sometime is a complete opposite. America's crime rate reflects a world of intimate violence where husbands kill wives for insurance money. Wives are cheating on their husband after encountering someone more handsome than their husband. Children become so rebellious that they barely listen to their parents. Hatred and jealousy become very popular among family members. Every day gives birth to a new plot against each other to bring them down or kill them. Women are desperately looking for protection from beatings or sexual assaults by their husbands or boyfriends. Each time we turn on our television, similar stories are broadcasting.

On her 18 years of marriage, a woman spent nights in the car just to avoid her husband, who she said would grab her by the throat and beat her after his drinking binges. One night, fed up with his violent outbursts and with nowhere to turn, she found herself at the Crisis Center for South Suburbia, which offers emergency shelter for victims of domestic violence. That is where she has stayed for the past four months.

We are only now beginning to realize that children are the forgotten victims of the violence which occurs between their parents. While a great deal of attention has been directed to women as the primary victims of domestic violence - and quite rightly so - the effects on children have been overlooked. In terms of attention in the literature, and in service provision as well, children appear on the bottom of the scale, below even the perpetrators of the violence, their fathers. Society continues to perpetuate the myth that children are untouched by the chaos happening around them in their family home.

In contrast, the small amount of literature now being produced affirms the thesis that children are profoundly affected by domestic violence. Living in a home where domestic violence occurs frequently has been equated with living in a war zone or being involved in natural disasters such as fire, earthquakes or cyclones. Children from violent homes can exhibit the same sort of post-traumatic stress disorder symptoms as child refugees from the Pol Pot regime in Cambodia or children living in Northern Ireland. However, the further complication associated with family violence is that it not only psychologically and sometimes physically harms the child victims, but also that it is likely to establish patterns of behavior which may persist through generations.

Relationships in the government

The U.S form of government is composed of the president, and the cabinet, including secretary of state. The cabinet should support the president and give him advice necessary for the success of the government. Sometimes we find the secretary of state or member of the cabinet resigns due to discord that's taking place among them.

Relationship at work

Work is very important in a society. We spend a lot of time at work, and our work is part of who we are. People are happy to go to work for so many different reasons such as to make money, make new friends and keep themselves busy as the day goes by.

Teamwork is highly recommended in a work place for the purpose of more productivity. We often find people grouped in different section in the work area working together to make the production more effective. We all deserve fair treatment and respect in the workplace. The working force is committed to your rights at work. We fight to protect these basic legal rights—like a fair minimum wage, workplace safety and freedom from discrimination. We also believe strongly in employees' freedom to form a union and collectively bargain, a right protected by the National Labor Relations Act.

Consequently, people bring all their personal views, experiences and approaches to the world with them to work. These things are very much a part of the talent people bring to their jobs. However, sometimes people have biases, prejudices or even just perceptions that lack some understanding, which can create conflict. These conflicts can be just from personalities, but often with America's diverse races, ethnicities, sexual orientations and immigrant populations, conflicts occur between people of different groups.

People's biases about race are older than America's history. However, deep rifts among co-workers and teams can occur when skin-deep issues surface. Co-workers may have feelings about each other's race or ethnic group--often founded in gross characterizations and stereotypes. Of even more intense concerns to companies, biases and even perceptions of biases among managers can be very problematic and legally devastating to a company.

Fifty years ago, classified ads in the newspapers listed jobs by men's and women's positions. The roles of women in the workplace were strictly defined and many professions were off-limits to women. Obviously, we have seen giant changes in the role of women in the American workforce.

However, not everyone agrees with all of the things that have changed. Not everyone believes in seeing women in all roles. This can be especially true regarding women in managerial roles.

Again, gender is a federally protected classification and companies must go to great lengths to assure that there is neither bias nor perception of bias.

More than ever, sexual orientation is a hot topic in workplace diversity circles. With states, including Vermont, allowing gay marriage and ongoing lobbying to give sexual orientation a federally protected status, organizations are giving increasing consideration to how to deal with the divisions society faces over homosexuality.

Even though federal law does not protect discrimination over sexual orientation, many states, counties and cities do. In addition, poor treatment or harassment by colleagues or managers can create legal exposure in civil court. These things can damage a workplace, morale and a company's reputation.

Relationship in school

School is a place where people receive instruction to be educated. People also learn new skills, find life time friends and acquire great memories. Public School in the U.S. refers to schools run by a governmental authority. In some states, such as Hawai'i, the state government runs all public schools; in others, local school districts run the public schools. States differ also in how public schools are financed. In general, they are financed from taxpayer dollars. Tuition to public schools is usually free; though parents are often expected to pay for some expenses as well as for optional programs like sports or music. Public schools may not deny admission to students based on academic criteria; they may expel and bar students for extreme disruptive conduct.

Private School refers to schools run by private entities, unaffiliated with the government. Private schools may set admission criteria, almost always charge tuition, and may offer religious instruction. Many private schools are run by churches or religious orders; these are known as parochial schools.

Public schools are generally prohibited from offering any religious instruction, a major source of controversy within the United States. In many locales dominated by one religious faction or another, there are frequent calls to "let God back in the schools". Neutral education on the subject of religion is permitted, as is the study of the Bible from a literary perspective; the prohibition is against favoring a specific religious view. Such decisions to remove God from schools offend the majority of religious people living in this country, and they tend to blame the government for the situation of the country going downhill and the violence in school as the result of that decision.

In general, school violence isn't easy to understand. There is no single reason why students become violent. Some are just following behavior they've seen at home, on the streets, or in video games, movies, or television. Sometimes, people who turn violent are victims of teasing who've hit a limit and feel like they would do anything to make it stop. They may feel isolated and rejected by their peers. These are only a couple of the reasons why a person may become violent.

After hearing news of school shootings or other violence, it's natural for students — no matter how old they are or where they go to school — to worry about whether this type of incident may someday happen to them.

When a tragedy like this happens, it's normal to feel sad and anxious, and to want to make sense of the situation.

Still, some schools have re-evaluated their safety needs in response to the concerns of families and communities. Some now require that guests check in at the office or have more guards on duty. Some schools have installed metal detectors.

Another thing that helps make schools safer is greater awareness of problems like bullying and discrimination. Many schools have started programs to fight these problems and to help teachers and administrators know more about protecting students from this type of behavior.

It's crucial to promote the importance of having the same mindset in relationship. Not only does it show a good image in our relationship, but also it becomes a healthy relationship, and more importantly, that is what God wants for us. For the Bible says, "the will of God will never take you where the grace of God will not protect you."(Psalm 91:1)

As we come to the end of the last chapter, we want to emphasize in our conclusion that the best way to think like Jesus is to surrender ourselves entirely to Him. By doing so, we create a baffle for God to take over and influence our mind. As the result, our mind will be Jesus's mind and we can call ourselves, "victorious, winners" in the name of Jesus.

REFERENCES

8 Surprising Health Benefits of Love
Discover all of the physical perks that come with a romantic relationship

http://www.womansday.com/health-fitness/wellness/a2306/8-surprising-health-benefits-of-love-1156 Copyright © 1998 - 2014 by Kent R. Rieske and Bible Life Ministries. All Rights Reserved.

How to Live a Joyful Life: 12 Ways to be Joyful, Christian Guide to Finding Joy & Staying Joyful; How to be a More Joyful Person or Christian, How to live Joyfully Bible Verses by Bomi Jolly

The Art of Learning How to Love by Joyce Meyer

Feeling unloved or unlovable? by Susan Gregg | Oct 14, 2013 |

Bible Verses to Show How Jesus Prayed by John Daniel

Unity and Great Teamwork By Jon Gordon

Unity of Christians by Paul Fuzier

Jesus Set the Pattern of Humility
Library:English Publications (2000-2015)

How to show empathy to others: 5 Christian ways by Dereek Hill

Why Helping Others Actually Helps Yourself BY KYLE ROBBINS

Biblical Ways to Handle Disunity By Rick Warren

What Are Some Diversity Issues Found in the Workplace & in America? by Eric
Feigenbaum

www.ingramcontent.com/pod-product-compliance
Lightning Source LLC
Chambersburg PA
CBHW070300290526
45791CB00003B/1025